TRAVEL ARIZONA

FULL COLOR TOURS OF THE GRAND CANYON STATE

ARIZONA
HIGHWAYS BOOK

Text by Joseph Stocker

Photography by
Arizona Highways
Contributors

Edited by Wesley Holden

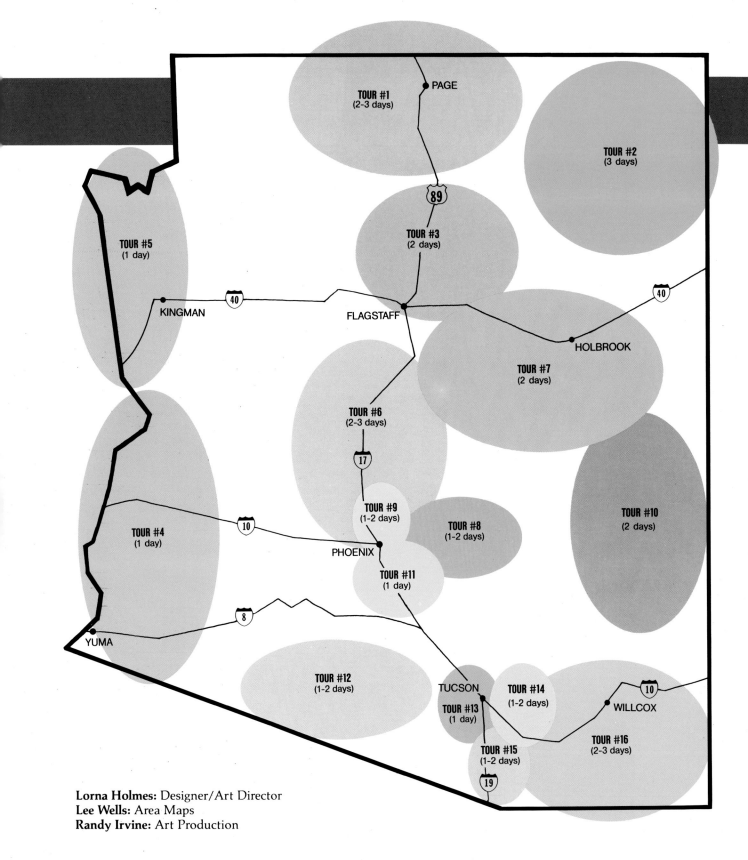

Lorna Holmes: Designer/Art Director
Lee Wells: Area Maps
Randy Irvine: Art Production

Travel Arizona was prepared by the Related Product Development Section of *Arizona Highways:* Hugh Harelson, Publisher; Wesley Holden, Managing Editor. Address correspondence to *Arizona Highways*, 2039 West Lewis Avenue, Phoenix, AZ 85009.© Copyright 1985 by Arizona Department of Transportation, State of Arizona. Third printing 1985. All rights reserved. Reproduction of the whole or any part of the contents without written permission of the publisher is prohibited. Library of Congress Number 83-071966. Printed and bound by Toppan Printing Company, Ltd., Tokyo, Japan. ISBN 0-916179-03-6.

Ilo & Ev Hendricks

Contents

Introduction

Arizona is a great big gorgeous state, and also a state of almost incalculable variety. Mountains. Canyons. Lakes. Rivers. Deserts. Indians. Museums. National parks. National monuments. Palm trees, pine trees, Joshua trees, and 76 species of cacti. And on and on and on.

Where to start? What to look for? Where to go and how to get there?

This volume attempts to answer those questions. We suggest that you take in Arizona's infinite beauty and variety in bits and pieces...systematized, coherent, well-laid-out bits and pieces.

And so, after much discussion, and based on a thorough knowledge of the state, the staff of *Arizona Highways* and the author of this book (himself a resident of Arizona for 40 years) have designed these 16 tours. They reduce the immensity of our state to manageable components. They provide you choices. And they also give you an opportunity to establish some traveling priorities.

We've carefully scouted each tour, measuring the mileage to keep the daily increments within reason and insure you the time to savor what you're seeing. Where, for example, we've suggested that a given tour can be negotiated in a day, we're talking about an easy-does-it day. No rush. No nervous clock-watching.

We've done some other things, too. We've made as many of the tours as possible into circle tours, so you can go one way and come back another.

Also we've kept pretty much to the main highways. Most people, we'd guess, prefer to do their traveling that way. Getting off the beaten track—a twisty trail to some distant canyon, a cowpath snaking out across the high

plateau—we've left for those gutsy folk with four-wheelers and high adventure on their mind.

There are, though, a few portions of our tours that take you off the pavement, as, for instance, the eastern part of the Apache Trail, between Phoenix and Globe. But it's well-maintained gravel, and, except in very bad weather (which, of course, we have very little of!), is eminently travelable. We are careful to stipulate where a tour takes you over a road that is not hard-surfaced.

So come see the kaleidoscopic diversity of this beautiful state of ours. Soak in its loveliness; thrill to its vistas. Stop often, to look and ponder and feel. And above all, drive carefully.

And now—come tour with us!

Joseph Stocker

(Front cover) Horizons seemingly recede to infinity in a moody view from Hopi Point in Grand Canyon National Park. Ed Cooper photo *(Above) Tinted by a famous Arizona sunset over rugged desert mountains, rain showers evaporate before they reach the ground.* Charles Busby photo

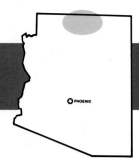

Lake Powell · North Rim

What better place to start touring Arizona than from the tip-top of the state? And what more gigantic and enticing piece of scenery to begin with than Lake Powell, which has become one of the most popular vacation areas in the state?

Powell is the centerpiece of the Glen Canyon National Recreation Area. It was created in the 1950s by construction of Glen Canyon Dam, the newest and perhaps the last of the large dams to be built on the Colorado River.

Lake Powell is 186 miles long, with 96 major canyons and 1960 miles of shoreline—that's over 800 miles longer than the California coastline. "You can spend a year on that lake and never see the same place twice," marveled one visitor.

If you're starting out from Flagstaff, the nearest sizable city, allow, say, two-and-a-half hours to cover the 129 miles (via U.S. Route 89) to Page, which is Glen Canyon's gateway town. If traveling from Phoenix, you'll need about five-and-a-half hours; from Tucson, the better part of a day.

Page, of course, didn't even exist until the dam was begun, and it is now a major northern Arizona community. You might pause there to take in the John Wesley Powell Museum, at 6 Lake Powell Boulevard. Powell was the colorful one-armed Civil War veteran who explored the Colorado in the 1860s and 1870s. The museum has some fine photographs of the canyons and the wild river down which Powell and his companions traveled—some of the areas subsequently covered as the waters rose to form the lake that bears his name. There's an early-day river-runner's boat at the museum, too, and a replica of a Powell boat used by Walt Disney in *Ten Who Dared*, a movie about the Powell explorations.

Down the hill out of Page, then, to the dam and, beside it, the spectacular bridge spanning the canyon. The dam rises 710 feet above the bed of the river and generates enough power to serve a city of 1.5 million people. The bridge is one of the largest steel-arch spans in the world, and there's no better way to view the dam than simply to park on either side and walk out on the bridge.

(Left) Mere specks in a sweeping aerial view, two small boats scribe arcs near Gregory Butte at Lake Powell, on the Colorado River above Glen Canyon Dam. The vast Glen Canyon National Recreation Area encompasses 1,255,000 acres under the jurisdiction of the National Park Service.
David G. Parker photo

(Above) Floating above the once wild channel first run in wooden boats by fearless Major John Wesley Powell in 1869, modern houseboaters enjoy all the comforts of home and the myriad inlets and islets of 186-mile-long Lake Powell. The meandering shore-line totals almost the length of the eastern seaboard of the United States. Jerry Jacka photo

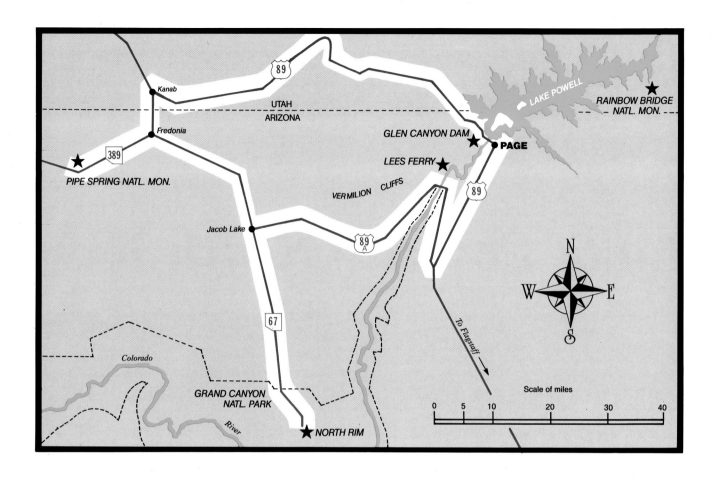

On the rim of the canyon above the dam is a Park Service visitors center from which you can take a self-guided tour of the dam. There's no charge.

From there it's only 4.5 miles to Wahweap, the principal recreational facility on Lake Powell. At Wahweap you get your first real panoramic look at the oh-so-blue waters of this second largest of America's artificial lakes (Arizona's Lake Mead being, of course, the first). Wahweap has just about everything the vacationer could need—a commodious lodge, campground, picnic shelters, beach for swimming, restaurants, and a large marina. This is where boat tours start, and there's a variety of them. You can tour Wahweap Bay aboard the *Canyon King*, a diesel-powered paddle-wheeler. You can rent a houseboat or a powerboat and go wherever you please and spend as much time as you want. You can take half-day and full-day trips aboard large power cruisers to Rainbow Bridge, 50 miles up-lake from Wahweap, past great fjords, red sandstone canyon walls, towering mesas, and sculpted palisades. (The full-day trip includes the exploration of a number of side canyons, some so narrow that there is barely room for a boat's passage.) At Rainbow Bridge you debark for a quarter-mile walk up to this largest and most magnificent of all the world's stone arches.

A cautionary note: you'll need reservations for just about everything at Lake Powell—accommodations, boat trips, boat rentals, whatever—particularly during the summer season.

Now head for the Arizona Strip, that spacious, barely populated stretch of outback reaching halfway across the state above the Grand Canyon. To get there, strike out southwestward from Page on U.S. Route 89, then turn north at the junction onto U.S. Route 89-A and cross the Colorado River at Marble Canyon. Navajo Bridge is every bit as dizzying as the one at Glen Canyon. There's more than one-twelfth of a mile of space between you and the river far below—467 feet, to be precise. At a settlement called Marble Canyon, a mile or so down the highway, take a right for the few miles of paved connecting road to Lees Ferry, which is notable for two things—what it used to be and what it is today.

What it used to be was a river crossing presided over by one of the West's most prominent patsies. That would be John D. Lee. He was one—but only one—of a group of frontiersmen who, at a place known as Mountain Meadows, jumped a Missouri wagon train transiting southern Utah in the summer of 1857. They killed just about every human soul present—120 in all. Lee fled to the Colorado to stay out of sight and ferry travelers across the river. During that time the crossing became famous as part of the Honeymoon Trail, traveled by devout young Mormon couples coming up from Arizona and headed for St. George, Utah, to have their marriages sanctified in the temple. (The one at Mesa, Arizona, hadn't been built yet. See Tour 8.) Eventually, though, word of the massacre leaked out and somebody had to

Rainbow Bridge, the world's largest natural rock span, fills the sky just north of the Arizona-Utah border. It was carved when an entrenched meandering stream found a shortcut across a horseshoe bend. The salmon pink arch of Navajo sandstone could accommodate beneath it the dome of the United States Capitol.
Ed Cooper photo

(Left) Whether daylight is bright or muted, the Vermilion Cliffs of far northern Arizona seemingly glow with inner incandescence. Rising steeply more than a thousand feet, the escarpment overhangs fields of weirdly shaped boulders which perch like toadstools on eroded pedestals. (Right) By contrast, the lush Kaibab National Forest graces the plateau which forms the North Rim of the Grand Canyon.
David Muench photos

be thrown to the federal wolves. Lee became the chosen one. He was duly executed by a United States firing squad.

Now to what Lees Ferry is today: it's the takeoff place for the increasingly popular river runs down the Colorado.

Drop by almost any day and you're likely to see a fleet of pontoon rafts and white-water dories poised for the plunge into the Colorado's rapids.

A recent addition to the Colorado River trips is a one-day raft float trip downstream from Glen Canyon Dam to Lees Ferry.

Something else to be marveled at in the vicinity of Lees Ferry: the Vermilion Cliffs, a great red gash of cliffside meandering westward more than 100 miles from there to St. George, Utah. When the sun glints off the cliffs just so, you see all the shades of red ever invented—burgundy, scarlet, crimson, and, yes, the red of blood itself.

If you have the time and would like to look at buffalo on the open range, pick up a southbound dirt road 14 miles west of Navajo Bridge for a 21-mile drive south to House Rock Buffalo Ranch.

The ground rises under you as you move on westward along U.S. Route 89-A. The terrain changes, the vegetation changes, and suddenly you're in pines atop a great forested dome— the Kaibab Plateau.

At Jacob Lake (there's a lodge and campground, if you'd like to put down for the night) turn south on State Route 67 for the 45-mile run to the North Rim of the Grand Canyon. That drive is one of the loveliest in the state— through thick forest, breaking out suddenly into great green expanses of meadow. It's all quiet and remote because

the North Rim doesn't get nearly the traffic that the South Rim does. Keep an eye peeled for deer—they often can be seen from the highway. And for the Kaibab squirrel, a white-tailed species that's found nowhere in the world save the Kaibab.

You're higher at the North Rim than at the South by some 1300 feet, which explains why the North Rim is closed in winter. It just plain gets snowed in. Interestingly, you're only nine miles by air, or 22 miles by foot or mule, from Grand Canyon Village on the South Rim, yet you have to drive more than 200 miles to get from one side to the other by car.

The principal North Rim drive is a 17-mile paved road out to Cape Royal. (There's a three-mile side trip from this road to a place called Point Imperial.) From Cape Royal you can look across one of the widest expanses of the Grand Canyon and pick out notable Canyon formations such as Shiva, Zoroaster, and Isis temples. And on a clear day, which is most of the time in this magnificent land, you can see San Francisco Peaks at Flagstaff, 70 miles to the south.

There's the standard Park Service charge for admission to the North Rim. And there are accommodations (lodging and campground), although not as extensive as at the South Rim. Reservations are suggested.

Back at Jacob Lake, go northwest 30 miles on U.S. Route 89-A, to Fredonia, then take State Route 389 west 15 miles to the western terminus of our tour — Pipe Spring National Monument. It was a ranching outpost established by Mormon settlers. A stone fort was built in 1873 for

(Left) Human scale is reduced to minuscule at the Grand Canyon, "the most revealing single page of earth's history...." Here visitors enjoy the dramatic views from Angel's Window, on the North Rim near Cape Royal. Dick Dietrich photo

(Above) Originally built by Mormons as protection against Indians, today Pipe Spring National Monument, serves as a living history museum.
Josef Muench photo

protection from Indian raids, and the first telegraph station in the Arizona Territory was installed here. A man named Anson Winsor built the fort, and so it came to be called—what else?—Winsor Castle.

And whence the name of Pipe Spring itself? Ah, therein lies another story. One of the early pioneers was William Hamblin, brother of Jacob Hamblin, Mormon missionary and confidant of Brigham Young (and, incidentally, the Jacob of Jacob Lake). Well, it seems that Bill Hamblin fancied himself quite the marksman. Somebody bet him he couldn't put a bullet through a silk handkerchief. He agreed to the bet—and lost. The ball merely brushed the silk aside instead of passing through it. So Hamblin took a clay pipe and placed it on a rock near the spring that flowed nearby. He said, "I'll shoot the bottom out of the bowl without touching the rim," and he did.

Today, guides, dressed in period costumes, show you the old hand-carved wooden bedsteads, primitive tools, and spring house where butter was churned and cheese was made. As you watch, they even quilt as was done a century and a quarter ago. What you see, in short, is how the Mormon pioneers persevered.

If you're going back to Page and would like a different route, backtrack to Fredonia on State Route 389, cut north to Kanab, Utah, (where many a Western movie has been made) and follow U.S. Route 89 back to Page.

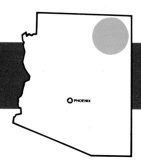

Navajo and Hopi Country

Fly over this northeastern quadrant of Arizona and you see a vast emptiness broken only by accidents of terrain—steep-walled canyons, squat sandstone buttes, and countless ranges of high desert mountains. Drive over this area and it appears, at first glance, to be just that again—sheer space and distance. Ah, but look more closely. There at the bottom of a broad valley or at the base of a hill or simply out in the middle of nowhere is a sign of life—a roundish dwelling. This is a Navajo *hogan* (the word means "my home"). It's six- or eight-sided usually, with its door facing east. For it is in the east that the Navajo gods gather, and the first waking view, therefore, is to the east.

This, then, is Indian land—Navajo and Hopi. The Hopi reservation is like an island surrounded by the Navajo sea. And that sea is a mighty one, covering more than 25,000 square miles of northeastern Arizona, northwestern New Mexico, and southeastern Utah—the largest of all Indian reservations. Navajoland alone is as big as West Virginia.

And it is not as empty as it seems. There are 150,000 Navajos living here, some in settlements and communities, many more singly and in family groups, their hogans often lying alongside more modern cement-block houses. As for generations past, sheep are still an important part of their sustenance. And so, when you see a hogan, you are liable to see, close by, a Navajo shepherd with her flock. (She will be standing there etched against the skyline, full-length Navajo skirt rippling in the wind that often whips across this spacious land.)

Times do change, though, even in what seems like a changeless region. And one of the major changes is accessibility for the tourist. Not too long ago only venturesome travelers embarked into Navajoland. Roads were bad, and accommodations scarce.

(Above) She has raised her sheep and shorn them; dyed and spun their wool. Now a Navajo weaver fashions an intricate design on her ages-old vertical loom.
Kathleen Norris Cook photo

(Right) Monument Valley forms a vast depression in the mile-high plateau country, and jabs the skyline with towering formations 250 million years old.
David Muench photo

(Above) Of three major cliffside villages protected within Navajo National Monument, Betatakin Ruin suggests a city of the future — improving its environment with an impervious dome. But Betatakin is old: A.D. 1250-1300. Ed Cooper photo

(Right) Keet Seel Ruin has 150 rooms still intact. Included is a ceremonial kiva (underground chamber) and a 35-foot-long Douglas fir beam used by the original Anasazi builders.
James Tallon photo

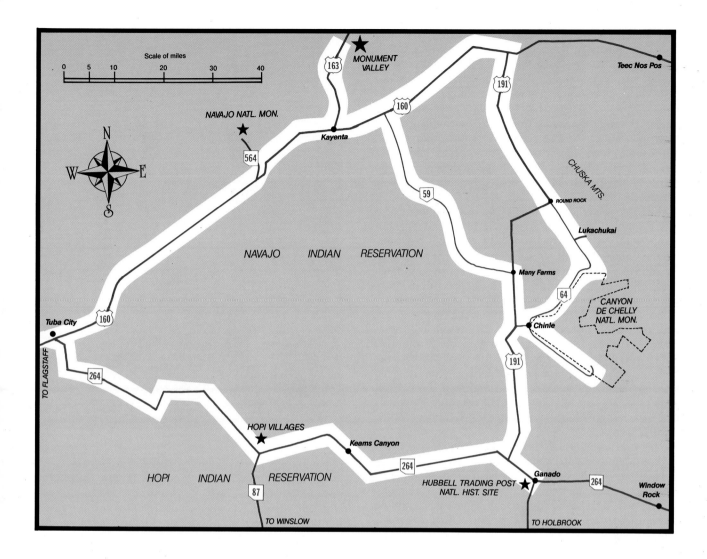

Today there are paved highways to practically anything you want to see, and there are good motels, too, some of them run by the Navajo and Hopi tribes themselves. Tourism, in a word, has become as important as sheep in the Indian economy.

What's more, some of the more sensational scenery to be found anywhere in Arizona—indeed, within the continental United States—awaits you. Connoisseurs of this sort of thing consider Monument Valley and Canyon de Chelly to be nothing short of spectacular!

When to see the Indian country? Late spring and early fall are best. Midsummer can get pretty hot here (although travelers still come in numbers, that being the traditional tourist season). And, since this is high country, winter can bring extreme cold and lots of snow.

Start your tour at Tuba City, a trading and tribal center in the western part of the reservation. It's 61 miles north of Flagstaff. So, if you're coming from Flagstaff, allow an hour or so travel time, and if from Phoenix, about four hours. And here is a suggested tour schedule:

Day One: On your way into Tuba City from the west on U.S. Route 160, keep an eye out for a turnoff—seven miles from town—to the dinosaur tracks. They're pre-

cisely that—footprints left by dinosaurs 180 million years ago in a mud flat which ultimately turned to rock. There's a picnic area nearby.

From Tuba City head northeast on U.S. Route 160 a distance of 54 miles to the turnoff northward on State Route 564, which takes you 9 miles to Navajo National Monument. This is a collection of three splendid prehistoric cliff dwellings— Betatakin, Keet Seel, and Inscription House. (The latter, at this writing, was closed for stabilization of the site and problems of access. The first two are open to the public.)

Get your bearings and some anthropological background at the visitors center. A short stroll from here takes you to an overlook for a distant view of Betatakin. The word is Navajo for "house on the ledge," and that's what Betatakin is—a cluster of dwellings tucked inside a huge cavern in the canyon wall. The people who lived here, some 700 years ago, anthropologists call Anasazi, which, in Navajo, means "the ancient ones."

In season (Memorial Day to Labor Day) there are ranger-led hiking tours of the ruins three times a day; in spring and fall, less often. The tour takes four hours and is quite strenuous—the equivalent, roughly, of walking down the stairs of a 70-story building and then back up again. But it's a rare opportunity to peer back into antiquity and see and hear how the Cliff Dwellers lived.

Keet Seel is even more demanding. It's eight miles out from the visitors center and then, of course, eight miles back...but well worth the effort! It's a veritable cliff village, the largest such dwelling in Arizona, with no fewer than 160 rooms. (Whether you go by foot or horseback, you need to have a reservation, since only 20 persons a day can make the trip. Write: Superintendent, Navajo National Monument, HC 63, Box 3, Tonalea, AZ 86044. Telephone (602) 672-2366.)

Upon leaving Navajo National Monument, return to U.S. Route 160 for the short run (a little over 40 miles) to Monument Valley via Kayenta and U.S. Route 163. Save for the Grand Canyon, probably no scenic attraction in Arizona — perhaps none in the United States — has been more photographed than this surrealistic outdoor wonder called Monument Valley. John Ford, the famous Hollywood director, filmed one Western classic after another here and, in the process, made Monument Valley internationally renowned. It was in one of the early Monument Valley productions of what film folk liked to call the "John Ford Stock Company" that John Wayne achieved stardom. And the tradition has continued through an endless succession of films and television commercials using the red-gold buttes and spires of Monument Valley as their locale.

This is not a national park but rather a Navajo tribal park, pridefully owned and managed by the Dineh themselves (Dineh is Navajo for "people"). The monuments become visible long before you get to the park, as you drive north on U.S. Route 163, passing such stunning formations as El Capitan and Owl Rock. At a crossroads a mile north of the Utah line, turn right to the visitors center. It's on a promontory, and from here you can see some of the more striking formations such as Left Mitten and Right Mitten (they do look like mittens, standing straight up) and several others. But you need to drive on into the park (there's an entrance fee) to view such celebrated monoliths as the Totem Pole (a miraculously thin spire rising 470 feet into the air), Three Sisters, the Big Hogan, and the arch known as Sun's Eye. As one tourist marveled, "There's no way you can explain this country to anyone. You have to see it!"

The monuments were formed by successive cataclysms of earth upheaval and volcanic eruption and then by centuries of wind-and-water erosion. Light, shadows, and perspective play gigantic tricks. What looks like an Indian chief may, as you move about, or as the light changes, suddenly become a dinosaur. And among it all are the wondrous colors — the red sand of the valley splashed with clumps of green growth and crystal-blue sky from horizon to horizon.

The road, while driveable in a family car, leaves something to be desired, and if you want to see the entire valley (and spare wear and tear on your car), it would be well to book a Jeep tour. Indeed, the farthermost reaches of this "Valley of the Giants" can be seen only through a guided tour (and the guides are, of course, Navajos).

(Above) One of the largest and best preserved ruins in Canyon de Chelly National Monument is the White House, occupied (according to tree-ring dating) by Pueblo peoples A.D. 1060 — 1275.
David Muench photo

(Right) Beneath an undercut 630-foot sandstone wall of Canyon del Muerto — a tributary of de Chelly — huddles Antelope House. It is named for Indian pictographs (in brown and white pigments) of the animals that were once so prevalent throughout the area. Jeff Gnass photo

Day Two: If you want to go directly to Canyon de Chelly from Monument Valley, there's a good paved road — Navajo Route 59 — across the reservation. It links up with U.S. Route 191 at Many Farms and then goes down to Chinle and out to the canyon. Or, if you have a little more time in your schedule, continue northeast out of Kayenta on U.S. Route 160, turn south on U.S. Route 191, and leave it at Round Rock for the road through Lukachukai that takes you into Canyon de Chelly via the north rim.

Canyon de Chelly National Monument (it's pronounced d'shay) is a magnificent mix of prehistoric treasure trove and geological wonder. Literally hundreds of Indian ruins, centuries old, are contained in a complex of canyons. The

TREASURES OF THE FOUR CORNERS

In the steps of the ancient ones

Text and Photos
by Carolyn Z. Roth

On the border of Colorado and Utah, Hovenweep National Monument contains numerous ruins of Anasazi towers. Hovenweep (Ute for "deserted valley") flourished at the same time as Mesa Verde.

(Clockwise from top) *Deep in magnificent Canyon de Chelly, Navajos farm where Anasazi farmed before them. A hiker investigates ruins in the Four Corners. Archaeologists work a dig in an effort to solve some of the mysteries about the ancient ones.*

CROSSING AN IMAGINARY BOUNDARY INTO THE REGION known as the American Southwest, you enter a place as culturally different from the rest of the U.S. as Asia or Egypt. For more than a millenium, various Indian cultures have lived, worked, worshipped, and died here, bestowing a distinctive ambience to the land.

The region known as the Four Corners (because the boundaries of four states meet here) is a melange of sights and experiences. In a single day you can drive through miles of empty silence, broken only by bold plateaus, massive sandstone monoliths, and red, red rock, or hike into a remote canyon, once the home of hundreds of cliff-dwelling Anasazi Indians. At a quiet, dusty pueblo you can see children playing on the flat rooftops or women baking bread in beehive-shaped earthen ovens.

Cortez, Colorado, is the ideal jumping-off point for exploring the Four Corners region. In a large valley among the mountains of the southwest part of the state, Cortez is a market town for nearby ranches. Tourism as well as exploration for oil and gas are important to its economy. Throughout the valley, you'll notice agricultural fields plowed or planted with crops, their rolling hills dotted with mounds of rock and rubble. Often, these knolls are all that remains of ancient one- or two-story Anasazi dwellings.

About ten miles north of Cortez on Highway 145, turn west on Highway 184 to visit the Anasazi Heritage Center. Here, amidst an impressive array of exhibits, interactive computer simulation programs, and hands-on activities like grinding corn on a real metate, you can immerse yourself in learning about the lifeways of the Anasazi people. Navajo for "ancient ones," the "Anasazi" enjoyed a highly developed culture and were possibly ancestors of today's Hopi and Rio Grande Pueblo peoples.

Operated by the Bureau of Land Management, the Heritage Center houses a collection of almost two million archaeological artifacts, documents, and samples. With computers, libraries, and collections, it will afford scientific study and research opportunities for many years to come. If you're interested in getting involved, ask about the museum's volunteer program. From unpacking and labeling thousands of fragile artifacts to working with school groups, dedicated volunteers contribute thousands of hours each year. Every bit of work done is a step toward solving the mysteries surrounding the Anasazi, and assuring that the irreplaceable resources they left behind are protected.

Outside the Heritage Center there is an interpretive trail leading to nearby Dominguez and Escalante Ruins, Anasazi dwellings that have been carefully restored by archaeologists. The view from the top of the handicapped-accessible hill is unprecedented. Tiny sandstone rooms and a great circular kiva are at your feet, and the valley stretches out far below in a wide panorama. To the south in New Mexico, the isolated volcanic plug called Shiprock sharply punctuates the flat expanse; to the west, the Sleeping Ute Mountain gently rises from the plain.

To see this vast quiet landscape now, the horizon intermittently broken by a ranch house or small community, it's hard to imagine that once many thousands of people lived here. Excavations show that 2,000 to 3,000 people lived in the Dolores River Valley alone in the ninth century. At that time, more people lived in some parts of southwestern Colorado than do now. Within a century, almost all the Anasazi were gone, a fact that perplexes archaeologists.

To feel the presence of these people who lived so long ago, it's best to visit first several sites that have been excavated by archaeologists and reconstructed so that you can see what they were like when the Anasazi lived in them. Then, when you visit the more remote locations, possibly untouched since the Anasazi walked away almost a thousand years ago, you can more easily imagine what the villages looked like.

ONE OF THE NATION'S LARGEST ARCHAEOLOGICAL preserves, Mesa Verde National Park protects a complex network of Anasazi ruins. Ten miles east of Cortez off U.S. Highway 160, a score of deep canyons seam the mesa. In the shelter of hundreds of caves eroded high in the rocky walls are some of the largest and best preserved Indian cliff dwellings in the world.

The earliest known inhabitants came to this area about A.D. 500 and built subterranean pithouses on the top of the mesas. For some unknown reason they moved into caves and built complex cliff dwellings during the thirteenth century. In the last quarter of the century a drought struck, driving the Indians from Mesa Verde to search for more reliable water sources.

Paved roads lead to many of the ruins, carefully excavated and meticulously restored throughout the park. Don't miss the Ruins Road, two six-mile loops that afford views of nearly forty outstanding cliff dwellings from canyon rim lookout points. Interpretive rangers lead guided walks into some ruins, permitting you to climb up ladders and enter the dwellings.

Although Mesa Verde is spectacular, visitors enjoy the less developed places as well. The ruins at Hovenweep National Monument, forty-two miles west of Cortez on the Utah-Colorado border, are truly remote, no matter how you look at it. All the roads into the Monument are graded gravel and dirt, and since they can become muddy and impassable during rainstorms, be sure to check weather conditions before venturing out.

Make time to go for a hike at Hovenweep. This Ute word meaning "deserted valley" seems well suited to this isolated land of mesas and secluded canyons north of the San Juan River. Standing on the edge of a mesa with the hot wind whipping through the junipers and pungent sage, you can easily imagine the bustling activity of a village nearby. In fact, if you look carefully, you can find the remains of check-dams where people trapped precious rainwater for their crops of corn, beans, and squash.

If you're an adventurous type, plan to visit Chaco Culture National Historic Park, about two and one-half hours south of Farmington, New Mexico. Definitely off the beaten path, Chaco Canyon is reached by traveling south on Highway 44, then southwest on Road 57 for twenty-five miles on gravel and dirt. So perplexing and unique was the complex civilization here, that archaeologists speak of its aspects as the "Chacoan Phenomena." The people set their planting and ceremonial calendars by observation of solar cycles and monitored the sun from a specially designed observatory atop Fajada Butte. They built straight roads hundreds of miles long, sometimes thirty feet wide, the beds scooped down to bedrock. And they engineered the construction of many "outlier" communities as far as 100 miles away, most of them from a single, standardized design. In some cases, the Indians had to travel more than seventy-five miles to cut trees for huge wooden support beams. At Chaco Canyon follow self-guiding trails through Pueblo Bonito and other ruins.

Another link between the mysteries of the ancient Anasazi and modern Indians is Canyon de Chelly (say "d'shay") National Monument in northeastern Arizona. Deep in the sheer, high-walled canyons east of Chinle off Highway 191, Navajo Indians live and farm the land. Numerous sites in the park demonstrate that the Anasazi lived here for 1500 years prior to the Navajo.

THREE GORGES CUT INTO THE 250-MILLION-YEAR-OLD red sandstone, a place that has been a Navajo fortress for over three centuries. You're welcome to drive around the top of the canyon, peer in at the overlooks, or take the two-and-one-half-mile trail to White House Ruin, but traveling down into the chasm requires the services of a guide—native or a National Park Service ranger—by foot, jeep, horseback, or surplus U.S. Army personnel carriers from the Korean War. In the canyon, there are tidy farms and orchards around red-

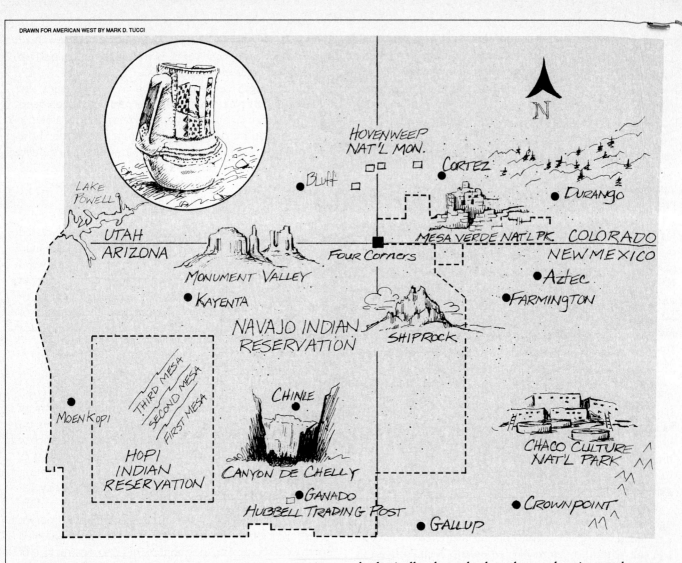

roofed hogans, bands of sheep, goats, horses, and the reddest slick-rock walls you'll ever see, some rising over 1,000 feet near the Lukachukai Mountains.

Not far south of Canyon de Chelly is 160-acre Hubbell Trading Post National Historic Site at Ganado on Highway 264. You can tour the grounds free and mingle with locals and other visitors while examining authentic Navajo rugs and crafts inside the ninety-year-old trading post. Much of the year, Indian women weave rugs on large looms in the adjacent museum.

Traveling west along State Highway 264 you'll enter the Hopi Indian Reservation, set in the midst of the Navajo Nation, considered by the Hopi to be the center of the universe. The Hopi live in a cluster of twelve villages off the highway, eleven of them atop or near First, Second, and Third Mesa. For bed and board, tribally owned and operated Hopi Cultural Center at Second Mesa has a motel and full-service restaurant. Here you can try traditional foods, including paper-thin blue piki bread, mutton stew, Indian tacos, and hot fry bread.

You're in luck if your visit coincides with a kachina dance, held February through August. At these colorful events, dancers adorned with masks, silver and beaded jewelry, their skin painted with crushed minerals, move rhythmically through the plazas chanting and singing hypnotically. These dances are religious services, so be considerate in your dress and actions. One important point to know is that the Hopi do not allow photography in any village—even photographs taken from the road are prohibited. Always ask for permission before taking pictures of Hopis or Navajos and realize that a tip is often expected.

To continue your visit in the world of contemporary Native Americans, venture into magnificent Monument Valley. The entrance is in Arizona, just south of the Utah line off Highway 163, north of Kayenta in the Navajo Tribal Park. There's a sort of raw beauty here—miles of open roads tempered by earthen hogans topped with TV antennas, children wearing Nikes, and elderly women sitting along the roadside dressed in traditional velveteen blouses and long skirts, selling cedar bead necklaces. Hundreds of movies and TV commercials have been filmed here. From sunrise to sunset, the massive sandstone buttes, fantastically eroded bluffs, and delicate arches strike an impressive scene of constantly changing color and character.

No doubt the scenery in the Four Corners will leave a lasting impression, but if you take the time and effort, breaking through to the heart of the native people is well worth the reward. As tenacious as the windswept country-

side, the people endure with a subtle sense of humor and pride as big as the land they live on. ✡

Carolyn Z. Roth *is a free-lance writer and photographer who lives in Oregon.*

Visitors investigate ruins of an Anasazi village in Frijoles Canyon, Bandelier National Monument, New Mexico.

WHEN YOU GO

Regarding accommodations in **Cortez, Colorado,** *consult the Cortez Chamber of Commerce, 210 East Main St., Cortez, CO 81321. Or call (303)565-3402.*

Crow Canyon Archaeological Center, *four miles from Cortez, offers week-long instructional programs where you can participate in archaeological excavation in remote Sand Canyon. Sessions run from May 28 through October 15. Cost is $690 for the first week and $620 for a subsequent week; college students pay $420. Fee includes meals, lodging, and instruction. Special symposia are more costly. Among them is a symposium tour of ancient Indian sites called "Three Worlds of the Anasazi," which will be offered October 1–7; cost is $995. For information write to Crow Canyon Archaeological Center, 23390 County Road K, Cortez, CO 81321. Or call 1-800-422-8975.*

Auctions of **authentic Navajo rugs** *take place at Crownpoint, New Mexico, throughout the year. Upcoming dates are July 14, August 25, October 13, and December 8. Crownpoint is located at the junction of New Mexico roads 9, 57, 371, northeast of Gallup and south of Chaco Canyon. Write to Crownpoint Rug Weavers, P.O. Box 1630, Crownpoint, NM 87313. Or call (505)786-5302.*

Camping *is available at most National Parks and Monuments. For information write to the Superintendent at each of the following:*

    Mesa Verde National Park, *Mesa Verde National Park, CO 81330*

    Chaco Culture National Historic Park, *Star Rte 4, Box 6500, Bloomfield, NM 87413*

    Canyon de Chelly National Monument, *P.O. Box 588, Chinle, AZ 86503*

    Hovenweep National Monument, *c/o Mesa Verde National Park*

   Anasazi Heritage Center, *27501 Hwy 184, Dolores, CO 81323. Or call (303)882-4811.*

   Hopi Cultural Center, *Box 67, Second Mesa, AZ 86043. Or call (602)734-2401.*

For information on tours, lodging and camping on the Navajo Reservation, write to **Navajoland Tourism Office,** *Navajo Nation, P.O. Box 663, Window Rock, AZ 86515. Or call (602) 871-6659.*

   Ute Mountain Tribal Park, *General Delivery, Towaoc, CO 81334. Or call (303)565-3751.*

   Hubbell Trading Post National Historic Site, *P.O. Box 150, Ganado, AZ 86505.*

JULY/AUGUST READER SERVICE

The advertisers listed below will send information to interested readers. Simply circle the corresponding number on the Reader Service Card and drop it in the mail to us. For those requesting payment, send a check payable to AMERICAN WEST for the proper amount to AMERICAN WEST JULY/AUGUST READER SERVICE, 7000 E. Tanque Verde, Suite 30, Tucson, AZ 85715. We'll forward all inquiries to the advertisers.

1. & 2. AMERICAN PAINT HORSE—Family horse, versatile, talented performance horse, a pleasure for leisure riding—the paint can do it all! Send for free information or $14.95 for a colorful, exciting, introductory video.

3. BED AND BREAKFAST, SANTA FE— Southwestern adobe bungalows to restored Victorian mansions, we offer a variety of settings and amenities. All located downtown, epitomizing the gracious personal attention of another era. Free brochure.

4. CARLSBAD CAVERNS, NEW MEXICO—Experience America's largest cavern by descending 750 ft. to the Big Room, or visit New Cave with flashlights, or discover the Chihuahuan Desert at the Living Desert, or relax on the Pecos River, or throw popcorn at a Melodrama, OR DO IT ALL!!! FREE info.

5. CATALINA ISLAND CRUISES—Largest Ships, Lowest Fares to legendary Catalina Island. Daily departures from Long Beach and San Pedro. Less than two hours away aboard spacious, triple-decked passenger ferries. For information circle Reader Service Card or call (213)514-3838.

6. CAXTON PRINTERS—Dedicated to the preservation of our heritage through literature for over 60 years. Backlist includes books on Indians, pioneers, outlaws, railroads, trails, ghost towns, and more. FREE catalog.

7. CEREMONIAL ASSOCIATION—Experience the tradition of the 68th annual Gallup Inter-tribal Indian Ceremonial, featuring the world's finest work by American Indian Artists. Circle Reader Service Card for more information.

8. CHAMA VALLEY, NEW MEXICO—Discover our native charm. There's something simple yet irresistible about northern New Mexico's Chama Valley. From fishing our lakes and rivers to hiking our trails, there's real adventure in our valley. You're gonna love the Chama Valley! Send for FREE information.

9. CHEYENNE OUTFITTERS—FREE WESTERN WEAR CATALOG. From the traditional to the latest fashion. Call (800)234-0432 for a full-color FREE catalog, or circle Reader Service Card.

10. CODY, WYOMING—Just an hour's drive east of Yellowstone through beautiful Wapiti Valley is the town where legendary Buffalo Bill Cody began his famous Wild West Show. Free brochures available.

11. CORTEZ, COLORADO—This archaeological center comes alive during Southwest Colorado's Colorfest. Spectacular fall foliage, culture, fun. Explore Anasazi cliff dwellings at Mesa Verde Nat'l Park or Hovenweep Nat'l Monument. Golf, fishing, water sports. FREE information.

12. CROW CANYON ARCHAEOLOGICAL CENTER, COLORADO—Work alongside archaeologists in the investigation of the vanished Anasazi peoples of the Southwest, or explore the ancient world of the Anasazi through an Anasazi Symposium. No experience necessary. Programs for students and adults. Free color brochure.

13. CUMBRES & TOLTEC RAILROAD—64 miles on America's longest and highest narrow-gauge steam railroad in the spellbinding southern Rockies. Running daily mid-June to mid-October between Chama, New Mexico, and Antonito, Colorado. Scenic thrills, tunnels, breathtaking trestles. Awesome fun! FREE brochure.

14. DAVID LIGHT—Quality fine art prints in the primitive tradition of Grandma Moses, Horace Pippin, and Manuel Lepe. Investment, pleasure, or a combination. David Lights prints open a rich and colorful world. Free information.

15. DURANGO, COLORADO—Authentic steam-powered, narrow-gauge train, ancient cliff dwellings at Mesa Verde National Park, Vallecito Lake, national historic districts, Victorian charm. Century-old saloons, melodramas and stage shows, great restaurants, shops. Accommodation Reservations: (800)525-8855, or (800)358-8855 (CO) Send for FREE information.

16. DURANGO & SILVERTON NARROW-GAUGE RAILROAD—Only regulated 100% coal-fired, Narrow-Gauge Railroad in the United States. Travels from Durango, Colorado, through the remote wilderness area of the San Juan National Forest to the old mining town of Silverton. Open May 6–October 29. Free information.

17. ESTES PARK, COLORADO—The "purr-fect" place (see ad, pg. 13). A wilderness recreational area for the whole family. Nestled in a verdant valley, gateway to Colorado's magnificent Rocky Mountain National Park. Enjoy an enchanting variety of shopping, dining, lodging, entertainment, and more! Free brochure.

18. FARMINGTON, NORTHWEST NEW MEXICO—The Navajos call it "totah," the meeting place of waters, which lies among mesas and rivers in the colorful land of the Navajo, Ute, Apache, and Pueblo Indians. Excellent year-round fly-fishing on the San Juan River. FREE brochure and maps.

19. FIDELITY COIN COMPANY—Coins for all purposes: investment, collection, etc. Money-back guarantee. Buy individually or in sets. Call (800)422-4733, or circle Card for FREE info.

20. FITZGERALDS CASINO/HOTEL—Your luck starts here! We offer you more ways to win, featuring the widest possible choice of games. Many are unique to the Fitz. Your satisfaction is our most important goal. Las Vegas' friendliest casino/hotel. Send for brochure.

21. FOUR CORNERS REGION—Ancient Indian ruins, contemporary powwows, breathtaking scenery, historic landmarks, and more! Experience the incredible diversity of the Four Corners, and remember it for a lifetime! Capture our magic in a fun-filled vacation with your family and friends. FREE brochures.

22. THE FRONTIER LIBRARY—Journey with us across the buffalo grass to the foothills of a time lost but not forgotten . . . relive the shining time of the mountain man through the pages of *The Frontier Library.* Send for free catalog.

23. GALLUP, NEW MEXICO, IS ADVENTURE—In the "Heart of Indian Country." Outdoor sports, recreation, history, attractions, and annual events amid awesome natural splendor. From the Sacred Mountains to Enchanted Mesa . . . SHARE THE SPIRIT. Circle Card for FREE colorful brochure. For poster (see pg. 21), call 1-800-242-4282.

24. GANDER MOUNTAIN—Providing merchandise for the serious, value-minded sportsman for 29 years. FREE catalogs featuring high-quality, namebrand outdoor equipment for hunting, fishing, camping, boating, reloading and more. Competitive prices; satisfaction guaranteed. Toll free order service.

25. GRAND CANYON WHITE-WATER RAFT... CANYON EXPLORATION—Enjoy the splendors of the Grand Canyon with our experienced guides. Trips include hiking, fishing, camping, excellent food. Discounts available. (602)774-4559 or circle Card for FREE information.

26. IDAHO'S CENTRAL ROCKIES—Four times the size of Yellowstone! Enjoy uncrowded scenic wilderness and world-class resorts. For FREE guides for recreation, lodging, camping, RV facilities, and Calendar of Events, call (800)634-3347 or circle Reader Service Card.

27. LA CUEVA LODGE, NEW MEXICO—GET AWAY FROM IT ALL! In the heart of the magnificent Jemez Mountains of New Mexico, this wonderful lodge offers excellent fishing, hunting, hiking, cross-country skiing, and much more. Business and group rates available. For FREE information, circle Reader Service Card.

28. LAS VEGAS, NEW MEXICO—Gunmen Billy the Kid and Doc Holliday hung out here in days past. Let history and architecture grab your imagination while golfing, fishing, hiking, and windsurfing. Las Vegas makes your New Mexico vacation complete! FREE brochures.

29. LINCOLN COUNTY, NEW MEXICO—In 1540 the first of the Spanish Conquistadores claimed these lands for Spain. Come see where Billy the Kid made his famous escape. Visit Smokey the Bear's Museum, Bonito Lake, Valley of Fires State Park, Ruidoso Downs Racetrack, and much more. FREE brochure.

30. LOS ALAMOS, NEW MEXICO—Gateway to the Jemez Mountains, set atop beautiful mesas, just 32 scenic miles from Santa Fe. Excellent outdoor activities. Ancient Indian ruins and modern pueblos nearby. Pleasant accommodations, restaurants, shops, museums. Free information.

31. MONTANA LAND—Own 20 acres or more in spectacular Montana. Unspoiled beauty, serene mountain settings, abundant wildlife. Fishing, hunting, snowmobiling—Montana is a natural. Send for FREE color brochure.

32. MOUNTAIN MAPS FROM HUBBARD!—Printed in color on durable plastic, raised relief maps with the detailed information of flat maps, plus an accurate, 3-dimensional scale model of the terrain that looks and feels real! FREE catalog.

33. MOUNTAIN PRESS PUBLISHING CO.—Expand your horizons through our broad selection of books on the American West, including Western history, Western Americana, the fur trade, geology, nature guides, and more. FREE catalog.

"This is war."

Fitness, concentration, nerves are only a few of the hurdles facing the contestants. Failure to heed the rules or familiarize oneself with an unusual artificial climbing surface may also derail the most promising climbing attempts. At Snowbird, French climber Didier Raboutou, who had finished the elimination-round route with almost two minutes to spare, marred his otherwise flawless performance in the finals by stepping over the boundary line that delineated the course from the rest of the climbing wall. He was later disqualified. Unaccustomed to the feel of artificial holds, American Ron Kauk, who had also given a stunning performance the day before, slipped when only twenty feet off the ground during the finals. This put him in last place.

Even with impeccable preparation, success "is due to sheer luck," remarks Fiona "Fizz" Atkinson. Her husband, British climber Martin Atkinson, routinely squeaks past the semifinal requirements but ranks in the upper half of most contest finals.

By 10:00 A.M. the day of the finals, sixteen pensive competitors (ten men and six women) who had been selected during the elimination rounds were "corralled" in a remote patio area. In isolation they could not hear descriptions of the route or benefit from seeing others climb. By noon, the remaining contestants were spastic with anxiety, yet the mood was gloomy. "It's like being led off to your execution," moaned one competitor. The last climbers remained in isolation the entire day.

Out in front, the day was sunny. Every fifteen or twenty minutes a new climber would appear, and although each contestant attempted the same route, there was much variation in style—in speed, fluidity, sequence, and of course, height. Each climber rendered an ad-lib vertical dance concluded by an inevitable plunge to the end of his or her rope.

At the 1988 Snowbird competition, climbers from France took the first three places in the men's division: Patrick Edlinger in first, Jean-Baptiste Tribout in second, Mark le Menestrel in third. After Britisher Martin Atkinson in fourth place, American men came in fifth, sixth, and seventh: Jason Stern, Christian Griffith, and Scott Franklin. Catherine Destivelle from France won first place among the women. Americans Mari Gingery and Lynn Hill tied for second, and Isabelle Patissier from France came in third.

After it was all over, the spectators shuffled off to their rooms and cars, gesturing and chattering excitedly. The effects of adrenaline-charged sport climbing had evidently spread among the audience. The competitors adjourned to the awards ceremony for plenty of wine and a long-awaited, full-course meal. Weeks of dieting went out the window this one night, for the following day they would be back at it. The next competition was two weeks away in southern France, and with a renewed sense of hope and a little more training, anyone could win. ✸

Catherine Gockley *is a free-lance writer and photographer who lives in Colorado.*

WHEN YOU GO

Snowbird Resort is just 31 miles southeast of Salt Lake City International Airport and 25 miles southeast of downtown Salt Lake City. Although rental cars are available at the airport, transportation to Snowbird from both the airport and downtown is available via taxi, shuttle service ($10 per person each way), and regular city bus. If you do drive up at night, watch out for deer—they're everywhere—as well as the occasional moose. Call Canyon Transportation at (801)255-1841 for airport shuttle information; (801)263-3737 for the Utah Transit Authority (bus service); or (801)521-2100 for Yellow Cab.

Snowbird is a first-class winter and summer resort situated in Little Cottonwood Canyon in the beautiful Wasatch Mountain Range at an altitude of 8200 feet. The resort offers a wide range of activities and amenities. Among summer activities are hiking, mountain bike tours, heli-golf, swimming, tennis, basketball, volleyball, and concerts by the Utah Symphony. Snowbird offers free guided hikes regarding the geology and history of Little Cottonwood Canyon. Rock climbing classes are available through the Mountaineering Center in the Cliff Lodge. A complete health and beauty spa is on the top two floors of the Cliff Lodge, while a fully equipped conference center adjoins the building.

Snowbird's fifteen restaurants and lounges run the gamut of cuisine, atmosphere, and cost. A wide range of shops provide hiking and ski equipment (for sale and for rent), high-fashion sportswear, jewelry, and gifts.

Snowbird has a capacity of 902 lodging rooms. Summer rates for 1989 range from $69 a night for a bedroom to $372 a night for a deluxe, two-bedroom suite. Rates are subject to change.

In 1989 the ISCC at Snowbird is scheduled for August 18–22. For more information call the Snowbird Resort at (801)742-2222; from Salt Lake City call 521-6040. For reservations only, call 1-800-453-3000; from Salt Lake City call 532-1700 for reservations only. For the Salt Lake City Convention & Visitors Bureau, call (801)521-2822.

As seen from a rim overlook, Spider Rock rises some 832 feet above the floor of Canyon de Chelly. By some accounts, naughty Navajo children are warned that their misbehavior will deliver them to a great spider which dwells atop the spire. Bob Clemenz photo

National Park Service administers the area, protects the ruins, and presides over the facilities that give visitors their access to this superb attraction. The Navajos—perhaps 40 or 50 families—live on the canyon floor. They move out in winter, but then in spring, when the snowmelt ebbs and the waters of Río de Chelly recede, they move back to grow their corn, squash, pumpkins, and peaches. From the towering height of the rim you can see their farms and hogans far below.

The Pueblo Indians left the canyon about 1350, after 30 years of drought, and the Navajos came just before 1700. They fought with successive waves of opponents—Spanish, Mexican, American. In one all-day battle, Spanish soldiers killed 115 Navajos who' had taken refuge in a rock shelter which now bears the name of Massacre Cave. You can see it from the north rim.

Motorized tours of the canyon floor are available and give you an intimate look at ruins that otherwise can be seen only from a distance through binoculars. Navajo guides take visitors in ex-military trucks of World War II and Korean War vintage. Park rangers also conduct hikes into the canyon from monument headquarters.

Day Three: Leave Chinle and head south on U.S. Route 191 to its junction with State Route 264. Go east a half-dozen miles to the Hubbell Trading Post. It's a national historic site dating back to the 1870s, when John Lorenzo Hubbell— Don Lorenzo to his friends—set up shop here to trade with the Navajos. Ultimately he and his sons came to own and operate 24 trading posts on the reservation. He saw himself not merely as a man with a business, but a man with a mission—to help the Navajos understand the ways of the white man, find markets for their products, counsel them, and help them when sick. When a smallpox epidemic struck in 1886 he turned his house into a hospital. He was immune because he'd had smallpox as a boy, but the Indians attributed his immunity to a higher power.

Hubbell died in 1930 and is buried on a hill behind his house alongside his wife and his closest Navajo friend, Many Horses. The trading post, open from 8 a.m. to 5 p.m., looks much as it did a hundred years ago. You can also take a ranger-conducted tour of the Hubbell home. The living room ceiling is covered with Indian baskets. Priceless Navajo rugs cover the floors. Drawings of Indians by famed artist of the period and friend of Hubbell, E. A. Burbank, adorn the walls.

Westward, then, on State Route 264, into the Hopi Reservation. The Hopi are a pueblo people tracing their ancestry to the cliff dwelling Anasazis. Unlike the nomadic Navajo who greatly outnumber them, they make more permanent homes. Their traditional homeland is a series of mesas—First, Second and Third—reaching out like giant fingers from the great Black Mesa to the north. On and about each mesa is a cluster of villages bearing such tongue-tangling names as Walpi, Shungopavi, Oraibi, and Hotevilla. The villages, with their stone-and-log houses, look much as they did centuries ago, although along the slopes below the mesas there are homes, stores, and schools of more modern construction.

You are welcome to drive up on the mesas and look around, providing you abide by the reasonable rules that

most spectacular of them, including multistoried apartments, perch within huge recesses in the vertical sandstone walls—walls that soar as much as 1000 feet above the canyon floor. Other ruins rest on the canyon floor itself. Most of them were built between A.D. 1100 and 1300, during the so-called Pueblo Period.

Along the north and south rims there are numerous overlooks that give visitors incomparable views of such major ruins as White House, Mummy Cave, and Antelope House. Signs posted at the overlooks send shivers through some viewers: *400-Foot Sheer Cliff. Control Children And Pets.* From White House overlook you can walk down a one-mile trail for a close-up inspection of this remarkable cliff dwelling. It's a relatively easy two-hour hike.

At the end of the south rim, at the junction of Canyon de Chelly and Monument Canyon, stands one of the most extraordinary monoliths in the entire Indian country—Spider Rock. As you view it from a 1000-foot overlook, you are a mere 200 feet higher than its top, for it rises 832 feet above the canyon floor.

Canyon de Chelly represents a kind of partnership between the federal government and the Navajos. The

the Hopi have posted on signs: *No picture-taking, sketching, or sound recording. No liquor. Respect privacy.*

If you're lucky, you might find yourself in Hopiland at the time of a ceremonial dance. Non-Indians may attend, although the dances are rarely announced in advance. They're usually on weekends. The most famous of them is the Snake Dance in August, in which the Hopi dance with live poisonous snakes in their mouths and somehow manage not to get bitten.

You can buy pottery and other craft art at private homes on the mesas. An array of crafts is also available at the Hopi Cultural Center on Second Mesa. Additionally, the center has a motel, restaurant, and museum (no charge). There's a motel, too, at Keams Canyon, a town east of the mesas.

The Hopi don't promote tourism as aggressively as the Navajo. But neither do they rebuff the tourist. They are a quiet, reserved, religious people living much as their ancestors did long years ago.

Drive on west of the mesas another 50 miles, or thereabouts, to Moenkopi, the westernmost Hopi village, close by the Navajo community of Tuba City.

(Above) Butterfly Dancers perform during ceremonials at Second Mesa, on the Hopi Indian Reservation. Villagers often have craft arts for sale. Jerry Jacka photo

(Left) Now a national historic site, Hubbell Trading Post at Ganado, deep within Navajoland, recreates an old-time mercantile operation, grocery store, and pawn shop. Weavers regularly demonstrate their skills. David Muench photo

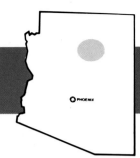

Grand Canyon · Flagstaff

Flagstaff is your base for this tour. If you're coming from Phoenix, add an extra two-and-a-half to three hours; if you're out of Tucson, an extra half-day or so.

Before leaving Flagstaff, you might want to take in a couple of interesting sights.

One especially worthwhile place to visit in this 7000-foot-high city is Lowell Observatory, tucked away in the pine forest on an eminence west of the downtown area called—appropriately—Mars Hill. It's an ancient-looking structure, with reason. Dr. Percival Lowell, of the famous family that included a long-time president of Harvard University (Lawrence) and a famous poet (Amy), founded the observatory in 1894. Some important work has gone on here, including the discovery of the ninth planet, Pluto, in 1930. The observatory is still very much in use. Lowell, incidentally, houses the world's largest collection of planetary photographs—some 2 million in all.

Outward-bound on U.S. Route 180, you might like to pause at a couple of exceptional museums. One is the Pioneers' Historical Museum; the other is the Museum of Northern Arizona. The latter features authoritative exhibits that portray the geology, biology, and anthropology of Northern Arizona and, along with all that, some excellent Indian arts and crafts. Its director proudly, and with justification, calls it "one of the gems of the museum world."

As you head on up U.S. Route 180, there is a particularly exciting view of the tallest of the San Francisco Peaks, Humphreys Peak. It is, at 12,670 feet, the highest point in Arizona. If you're traveling past the peaks in late autumn, you'll see great swatches of yellow on the slopes. Those are clumps of aspen that have turned with the first chill breath of oncoming winter. When winter arrives there's skiing at the Snow Bowl, high on the mountainside. Late spring covers the slopes with wild flowers.

It's 82 miles from Flagstaff to the Grand Canyon via U.S. Route 180, through rolling hills covered with bunch grass, junipers, and desert shrubs. Thirty miles south of the Canyon you join up with State Route 64 running north from Williams. As with all national parks, there's an admission charge to the Grand Canyon.

(Left) At Mather Point on the South Rim, the Grand Canyon gives meaning to the words of historian J. Donald Hughes: "Man has always found the Canyon mysterious, filled with awe-inspiring power, strangely attractive and repelling, beautiful and charged with meaning."
Dick Dietrich photo

(Above) A winter sunset tints the slopes of Arizona's highest mounts, the San Francisco Peaks, so high they harbor a swatch of Arctic tundra.
David Muench photo

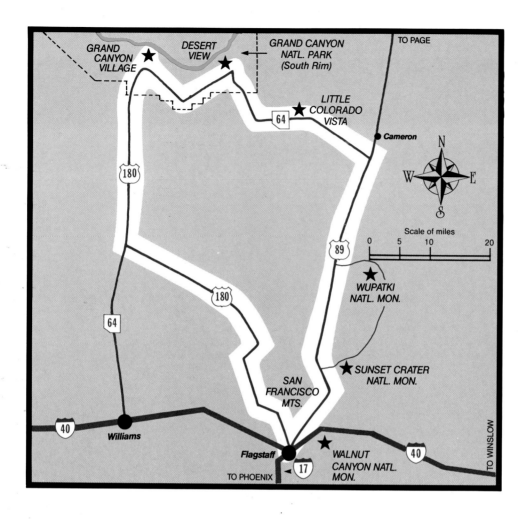

(Right) Prime range of the Rocky Mountain mule deer is the northern Arizona uplands. The area was a favored aboriginal hunting ground for a thousand years or more before arrival of Europeans.
James Tallon photo

(Following panel) Sunset spreads a spectrum of color across the Grand Canyon's South Rim near the Desert View Watchtower, an early tourist attraction.
Ed Cooper photo

You'll want to get your first view of this most wondrous of American scenic attractions at Mather Point, where the highway turns toward Grand Canyon Village. Strung out westward and eastward from there is an array of viewpoints. From some you can see the silver ribbon of the Colorado River winding through the gorge an unbelievable three-and-a-half miles beneath and beyond your feet. Stopping at all or most of the lookouts is by no means redundant. Each gives you a different aspect of the Canyon, different lighting, different juxtapositions of shadows, different moods.

There's a broad view up and down the Colorado from Yavapai Point, west of Mather Point. This is also the terminus of a nature trail that starts from the visitors center at park headquarters. Natural features are keyed to a printed guide. A museum is located here and another is at Yavapai Point, the latter with a scope fixed on various geologic formations in the Canyon. In season, rangers give daily lectures at both museums. A slide show at the visitors center and videotape at Yavapai Point explain the geology, life zones, and habitation of the Canyon.

You can, of course, drive from one point to the next. Or you can take a two-hour narrated bus tour along the West Rim or a three-hour bus tour along the East Rim. The westernmost viewpoint is Hermit's Rest, where there's a unique cliff house built of natural stone from the Grand Canyon. (Only motorized access to the West Rim and Hermit's Rest in summer is by free shuttle bus.)

Given stamina and surefootedness, you might want to consider hiking at least part way down into the Canyon, via Bright Angel or South Kaibab trails. (For hiking overnight, you'll need a permit from the Back Country Reservations Office near Mather Campground.) And then, of course, there are the famous mule trips, although either excursion—mule or foot—will keep you at the Canyon longer than the time we've built into this two-day tour. Reservations for the mule trip should be made well in advance.

On Day Two you might begin by exploring the village. Stop in at the famous El Tovar Hotel (some 80 years old) and the Hopi House, an authentic reproduction of a traditional home on the Hopi Indian reservation. You might also take in the museum in nearby Bright Angel Lodge, which displays, among other things, photographs of eminent guests.

Then head out along East Rim Drive. Viewpoints include:
• Yaki Point, thrusting out into the gorge, lets you swing around a 200-degree arc as you soak in the Canyon's infinite loveliness.
• Moran Point, offering an especially delightful view late in the afternoon when the shadows grow long. You look down on Hance Rapids, five miles to the northeast.

(Above) Phantom Ranch, one vertical mile down from the South Rim of the Grand Canyon. There are cabins, dormitories, a dining room, and a snack bar serving mule riders, hikers, and those who just come to absorb the grandeur.
Ed Cooper photo

(Right) Bright Angel Lodge is one of six lodges at the South Rim's Grand Canyon Village. Open the year around, they provide guests an opportunity to see the canyon in all its seasonal moods.
Thomas Ives photo

• Lipan Point, considered by many to be, among them all, the most beautiful vantage point.
• Navajo Point, a mile more to the east.
Lastly there's Desert View. You can look both ways from Desert View because it's above the apex of a right-angle bend in the Canyon. There's a 70-foot stone watchtower here, built by the Santa Fe Railroad in 1932. It has a glass-enclosed observatory equipped with powerful telescopes. This is the highest point on the South Rim. (Another campground is located nearby. It's first-come, first-served. And there are two more campgrounds outside the park. Caution: campground rules may change.)

About four miles east of Moran Point, you can see the remains of an 800-year-old Indian village—Tusayan Ruins. With it is a small museum open during the summer. There's no admission charge.

Then eastward out of the park, past a viewpoint that gives you a positively electrifying look into the depths of the Little Colorado River Canyon (not recommended for acrophobics!). In recent years a kind of Indian crafts market has developed right there at the gorge outlook— Indians selling their jewelry, rugs, and other crafts at enticingly low prices...and they take credit cards.

State Route 64 runs into U.S. Route 89 just south of Cameron, a trading post, and you head south about 20 miles before leaving U.S. Route 89 for a semicircle tour of Wupatki and Sunset Crater national monuments. Wupatki is an assemblage of ruins built by Indians who resettled this area during the 12th and 13th centuries. The area flourished at that time because the soil had been made fertile by the volcano we call Sunset Crater. It erupted and deposited a billion tons of lava and ash over the countryside. The largest of the Wupatki pueblos was three stories high and contained more than a hundred rooms. Wupatki is the Hopi word for "tall house."

Then on around the half-circle to Sunset Crater. (It got its name in modern times from the red and yellow colors of the rim.) The eruptions that created the crater occurred— or so we can infer from tree-ring studies—in the winter of 1064-65, about the time of the First Crusade. Marked paths lead you to interesting sights in the area. There's also a small campground. Both Sunset and Wupatki have ranger-staffed visitors centers with fine displays explaining the monuments.

You emerge through Bonita lava field which looks like something straight out of Dante. Join up again with U.S. Route 89 and head south, but instead of returning to Flagstaff, turn onto Interstate 40 east and drive a few miles to the Walnut Canyon National Monument turnoff. (There is an admission charge here, although none at Wupatki or Sunset.)

Within the horseshoe-shaped confines of 400-foot-deep Walnut Canyon are the remains of more than 300 small cliff dwellings. They were occupied some 600 years ago by a people we know as the Sinagua. It was a hideaway for them in an ideal environment, including a dependable water supply from Walnut Creek, a potpourri of plants and animals, and solid caves and ledges for building their masonry homes.

The Sinagua stayed around for about a century and a half and then disappeared. Nobody knows why or whence. Their cliff dwellings remained hidden there in Walnut Canyon until Lieutenant Edward F. Beale found them in 1858.

You can view some of the cliff dwellings from the Rim Trail or hike down Island Trail to see them close-up. It's a 185-foot descent by stairs and paved walks and takes a bit of doing, since, to cite a variation on that ancient theme of physics and economics, who goes down has to come up.

Back to I-40, then, and westward into Flagstaff.

(Left) Sunset Crater National Monument. This dormant volcano erupted in A.D. 1064-65 spewing lava, rock, and cinders. The debris dramatically altered the environment, changing it into a fertile farmland for ancient cultures.
Jerry Sieve photo

(Right) Walnut Canyon, home of the Sinagua people about 800 years ago, today shelters the evocative ruins of their cliff dwellings.
Bob Clemenz photo

(Below) Also inhabited by the Sinagua, Wupatki National Monument contains some 800 separate ruins. The area was a melting pot for early cultures who farmed the cinder-covered topsoil after the eruption of Sunset Crater.
Dick Dietrich photo

PHOENIX

Lower Colorado River

You can find bigger rivers, wider rivers, more spectacular rivers than the Colorado, but you can't find a more used and useful river. The lower Colorado, made supremely functional by a ladder of dams stretching from Glen Canyon in northern Arizona to Morelos Dam south of Yuma, transforms Arizona and California deserts into rich food baskets. It provides the watery wherewithal for fishing, boating, and swimming all up and down the western edge of our state—the Arizona Coast, as some call it. And, inevitably, people migrated here by the thousands to visit, to sightsee, to have aquatic fun and, in many cases, to make new lives along the shores of this busy river and the big blue lakes created by its dams. Brand-new communities have popped up out of nowhere, drawing sustenance from the Colorado. And almost all of this happened since World War II.

Yuma, a town rich in historical lore, is the southern anchor of what we might call Lower Colorado Country. It's a river town (actually a two-river town, since it is located precisely at the confluence of the Colorado and

(Right) A land of contrasts. The waters of the Colorado River, dammed and diverted, have turned a desert wasteland, near Yuma, into a fertile oasis where a multitude of crops are grown year-around. Jerry Sieve photo
(Inset, right) Interstate 8 today crosses the miles of dunes near Yuma, but in the 1920s the dunes were the site of a narrow plank road made of railroad ties held together with steel bands. Dick Dietrich photo
(Inset, far right) The London Bridge at Lake Havasu City arrived on the Colorado River's shore in 1968. Reassembled like a giant jigsaw puzzle, it quickly became one of Arizona's more popular tourist attractions. Carlos Elmer photo

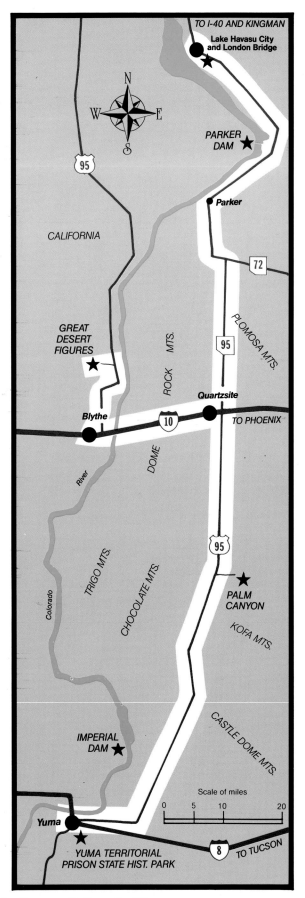

the Gila), and it is a commercial center (the traditional halfway point between Phoenix and San Diego). It's an agricultural city. It's a resort city (Yuma receives 93 percent of all available sunshine and is usually a few degrees warmer than Phoenix and Tucson). And it's a place with things to see, historical and otherwise.

The best-known attraction—made so by countless movie and television Westerns—is the Yuma Territorial Prison, now a state park. Situated on a rocky bluff overlooking the Colorado River, the prison served to keep the frontier's bad men (and a few bad women) out of circulation. Buckskin Frank Leslie, who contributed bodies to Tombstone's Boothill Cemetery, was part of the select company at the Yuma prison. So was "Heartless" Pearl Hart, a female stagecoach robber regarded as no lady by lawmen.

The prison was a dread place. The general idea was that one sojourn at Yuma prison would persuade a sinner to go forth and never sin again. Cells were lined with iron bands to discourage digging out. The unrelenting heat of a Yuma summer sent temperatures soaring to 120 degrees. There was a dungeon known far and wide as the "snake pit," even though it had no snakes.

Inevitably inmates of the prison preferred to be somewhere else, and some of them tried to get there. The most famous break of all was one in which the warden's wife, of all people, turned out to be the heroine. When several convicts took off for freedom, she helped operate a Gatling gun in the tower and frustrated the breakout.

Yet, for all its sinister reputation, the Yuma prison had its benevolent side. Food was nutritious...cells were ventilated...inmates could get an education...not bad for territorial days in the Southwest.

There's a small admission fee.

The Century House Museum at 240 South Madison is also worth seeing. Built in the 1870s, it was the home of a pioneer merchant, E. F. Sanguinetti, and is now a regional museum of the Arizona Historical Society. You'll enjoy photos, artifacts, and documents from Yuma's early days, along with pretty gardens and aviaries with talking birds. No charge for admission.

There are two things across the Colorado to see—the Quechan Indian Museum and the famous sand dunes where Hollywood has been shooting its *Beau Geste*-type movies since film was invented and, more recently, a lot of TV commercials. (And you thought those desert films were actually made in the Sahara!) The Quechan Museum marks the site of old Fort Yuma, one of the oldest military posts of the territory. This is also headquarters for the Quechan Indian tribe, and there are photographs, crafts, and artifacts to acquaint you with the Quechan and Cocopah Indians. There's a small admission charge.

Heading north out of Yuma on U.S. Route 95 you can see the first of the major Colorado River dams—Imperial—by leaving U.S. Route 95 about 20 miles north of Yuma for a five-mile detour westward to the river. The dam feeds the great canal system that waters California's immensely fruitful Imperial Valley. Three miles on to the north there's another side road, this one to Martinez Lake. It's a favorite close-in spot for fishing, boating, and waterskiing.

Another 40 miles to the north is the turnoff to Palm Canyon, about nine miles east of U.S. Route 95 on a gravel road. Palm Canyon is in the Kofa Mountains, in the western part of the Kofa National Wildlife Refuge, and is the only place in Arizona where native palm trees grow. All the rest of our palms are transplanted from places like southern California and the Middle East. Botanists say the palms have been growing in Palm Canyon for centuries and may have originated with the droppings of birds carrying seeds from California trees.

Be advised, though, that there's some walking involved. It takes about a half-hour to negotiate a gradual uphill path to a point where the main group of palms can be seen in a cleft in the canyon. A hike into Palm Canyon is not recommended during hot months.

The Kofas are also home for bighorn sheep. They're skittish creatures, and you may not see any.

Back to U.S. Route 95 and on north another 18 miles to Quartzsite, at the junction with Interstate 10, the Phoenix-Los Angeles freeway. Visit Quartzsite in midwinter and you won't believe your eyes. Spread out across the desert is a veritable ocean of motor homes, mobile homes, trailers, pickup trucks, tents, and what-have-you. Quartzsite has a population of about 450 in summer and 10-20,000 in the winter. People just drive out here and put down, because it's warm, free, and friendly. There's no water or electricity — folks bring their own. What happened, apparently, is that word has spread across the country that Quartzsite is the place to head for when the snow flies.

In February there's a big rock-and-mineral show that attracts 100,000 or more people and gets national publicity. Rockhounds come from everywhere to buy, sell, and trade their gemstones and whatever.

You might keep an eye out, also, for an unobtrusive gravesite that marks one of the more eccentric episodes in Arizona's history. It's the Hi Jolly monument which honors, interestingly enough, a camel driver. He actually was named Hadji Ali (you can see how it would come out, in Americanese, as Hi Jolly). Back in the 1850s the Army, in a unique experiment, imported a batch of camels from the Middle East to transport materials across the Western desert. With them came some native camel drivers, including Hi Jolly. During the Civil War the experiment foundered. Most of the drivers, homesick and bewildered by this alien land, went home, but Hi Jolly stayed. Some camels were turned loose into the desert. Hi Jolly became a prospector, and when he died, he was buried in Quartzsite cemetery.

Before you resume your journey north on State Route 95, you may want to consider a detour westward to Blythe, California, on I-10, to view one of the more intriguing archeological curiosities in the West...the Great Blythe Intaglios.

They're engraved into the earth, first discovered from

the air 40-odd years ago. And they're huge. One is an effigy of a human 170 feet tall (or, rather, long, since the intaglios are horizontal carvings), its spread-out arms measuring 160 feet from finger tip to finger tip. Another is an animal 53 feet long and 40 feet tall.

The large animal seems to be a horse, although Mohave Indians living in the area think it may be a mountain lion. The human figure, say archeologists, may be a mythological giant known as Ha-ak who ate children and was eventually chased away by an Indian brave.

Blythe is 19 miles west of Quartzsite. The turnoff to the intaglios is 16 miles north of Blythe on U.S. Route 95. Watch for a stone monument with a bronze plaque on the right side of the road. You'll only have to go a quarter-mile from the highway.

Twenty-three miles north of Quartzsite you join up with State Route 72. Another 12 miles and you're in Parker, which is the gateway to the lake country. En route you pass through the Colorado River Indian Reservation, which accommodates members of no less than four tribes —Mohave, Chemehuevi, Hopi, and Navajo (the latter two far removed from the main bodies of their tribes in northeastern Arizona). You should stop and take a look at the Colorado River Indian Tribes Library and Museum, located two miles south of Parker. It depicts centuries of Indian civilization along the river, and there's no charge.

Eight and a half miles north of Parker you come to La Paz County Park, a 540-acre outdoor recreation area with 4000 feet of Colorado River beach frontage. There are boat ramps, campgrounds, ramadas, and the like. About three miles farther and you're at Buckskin Moun-

tain State Park, which is more of the same and a good deal bigger, a hefty elbow of land jutting into the Colorado.

The big annual event in these parts (and it's really worth timing your visit to see) is the Parker Enduro, a seven-hour motorboat race held usually on the first Sunday in March. And what boats! They include the world's fastest inboards, outboards, and jetboats, doing 60 laps up and down a 13-mile stretch of water at speeds in the neighborhood of 125 miles per hour. It's the longest endurance race in the world, the granddaddy of power-boat marathons. It starts from La Paz County Park and runs south to Blue Water Marine Park, and if at all possible you should be on hand at 8 a.m. for the roaring takeoff. You'll have plenty of company. Thirty thousand to 40,000 people, complete with recreational vehicles (RVs), pickups, and just plain automobiles, line the banks of the Colorado to watch the Enduro.

In June there's another event that's a bit less exotic but gets a lot more people involved. It's the annual seven-mile Colorado River Innertube Race. Awards are given to everyone from the winner of the race to the one who finishes last and the one who wears the worst looking hat.

About 20 miles more and you're at Lake Havasu City, a town built out of nothing save desert, water, and a bright idea. It's located on the shores of Lake Havasu, which is the Colorado River backed up by Parker Dam. The man who had the bright idea was Robert P. McCulloch. He decided, back in the 1960s, to move his big chain saw factory out of Los Angeles to a climate healthier for employees and business. In order to do so he got some land on Lake Havasu and started himself a city.

Public-relations-conscious tycoon that he was, McCulloch then came up with another idea. He heard that the London Bridge was for sale. So he bought it, paying $2.46 million for the bridge and another $5 or $6 million to transport it stone by painstaking stone to Lake Havasu City for reconstruction.

There was a bit of English resentment at first. "Hitler Couldn't Get It, But McCulloch Has!" read a spray-painted sign near the 140-year-old bridge before its removal. Still, in the spirit of hands-across-the-sea and all that sort of thing, no less a personage than the lord mayor of London came over to take part in the ceremony that attended the laying of the first transplanted stone.

The bridge is now a major tourist attraction. An international village of European-style shops and Old World architecture has sprung up around it. And the publicity it has engendered, combined with the desert-versus-blue-water allure of the town itself, has caused Lake Havasu City to grow swiftly to one of the dozen or so more populous communities in the state. (There's an annual London Bridge Days celebration in early October—10 days of English-type festivals and contests, water sports events, arts and crafts displays, big-name entertainment, and folks dressed up in Elizabethan and Victorian costumes. Former lord mayors of London and their ladies make a special trip from England to Lake Havasu City to participate in a stately hands-across-the-sea-and-the-desert ceremony. Two other major annual events are the Lake Havasu Classic speedboat races Thanksgiving weekend and the big Chili Cookoff in early April.)

Just south of the city is Lake Havasu State Park—45

(Opposite page) An aerial view of giant intaglios etched into the desert pavement north of Blythe. These ancient figures remain a mystery to modern man. How did the artists that made them achieve the necessary altitude to execute the design? Does this grand scale art have religious significance? Is it related to the Mohave Indians' myth about a giant? These and other questions still puzzle anthropologists.
Wes Holden photo

(Above) The Great Colorado River Inner-tube Race at Parker draws thousands of river rats for the wet and wild competition each spring. Officials award prizes not only for the fastest tuber, but for best costumes, and most unique craft too.
Alan Benoit photo

miles of shoreline, beaches, boating and camping facilities, golf, tennis, RV centers, and the like. A big annual event hereabouts is the Lake Havasu Regatta—world's largest inland sailing competition. And in summer there are all manner of water sports competitions—sailing, windsurfing, jet skiing, Hobie cat racing. Then, come London Bridge Days, Havasu folk put on a super-duper water ski show called Excalibur.

If you're moving on to Tour 5, Lake Havasu City is a good place for staying the night. Lots of facilities.

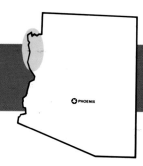
Northwestern Arizona

(Above) An egret, one of 60 species of waterfowl that frequent the lower Colorado River, takes flight from the marshlands lining the river's edge. James Tallon photo

(Right) In spring poppies, phacelia, ghost flowers, and a hundred other varieties of wild flower carpet the desert country of Lake Mead and Lake Mohave. These two huge reservoirs and the 2300 square mile Lake Mead National Recreation Area surrounding them combine to form a sun-filled watery wonderland where more than 5 million fishermen, waterskiers, pleasure boaters, hikers, and sightseers flock each year. David Muench photo

You now enter a region of extremes—sand contrasted with water, flinty desert contrasted with colossal man-made lakes. There's the hustle of the hurried motorist heading toward or away from Los Angeles, along one of the busiest interstates in the nation, and not far away, on a strip of quiet water between two canyon walls, sits a fisherman at utter peace with the world.

Much of this northwest corner of Arizona is contained in what the government administers as Lake Mead National Recreation Area. It encompasses both lakes—Mohave, backed up by Davis Dam, and Mead, contained by Hoover Dam.

There are some delightful things to see, though, before you reach the lower end of the Lake Mead National Recreation Area. Heading out of Lake Havasu City, you link up with Interstate 40 at a point 21 miles north. Drive west, then, some nine miles to Topock to gain access to a unique bit of landscape known at the Havasu National Wildlife Refuge. With patience, a little bit of luck, and a good pair of binoculars you're liable to see some of its 260 different species of birds, 40 species of mammals, and 20 species of reptiles. They include such rare types as the bald eagle, desert tortoise, desert bighorn sheep, and peregrine falcon.

A modest little craft, the canoe, is the way to go, in case you'd like to take the time. On the Arizona side of the Colorado, just southeast of Needles, California, is a piece of water known as Topock Marsh. Here, along about February, you can see many of the birds that migrate north along the Colorado River Flyway. The segment of river below Topock is known as the Topock Gorge, a 15-mile stretch of gentle water and incomparable scenery that seems to have been invented for canoeing. (Canoes can be obtained at Topock and arrangements made to pick you up at the end of your trip.)

Leave the interstate before it crosses the Colorado and head north on State Route 95 as it moves beside Topock Marsh, through a settlement called Golden Shores, and through the Fort Mohave Indian Reservation. What you're entering now is one of Arizona's newest boomtown areas.

Its population is exploding for as diverse a set of reasons as could be imagined: fishing, gambling, and just plain get-away-from-it-all living.

Fishermen from all over the country come here for the striped bass, and they catch some big ones! Not long ago the largest striped bass ever caught in inland waters was landed hereabouts, weighing in at an unbelievable 59 pounds 12 ounces.

The gambling is at Laughlin, Nevada, across the river from Bullhead City, Arizona. There are seven casinos in Laughlin, but most of the people who work there reside on the Arizona side of the river. They commute, as do the patrons of the casinos, via the free 24-hour ferry service across the river. (It's an eight-mile drive to Laughlin, over Davis Dam and back on the Nevada side of the river.)

Bullhead City got its start, in point of fact, from the building of nearby Davis Dam in the 1940s. The town's name came from a large rock shaped like the head of a bull which, ironically, disappeared after the dam was finished and the waters of newly-created Lake Mohave rose. Everybody figured that when the dam was done, Bullhead City would fold up. But it didn't. It grew, thanks to that unfailing mix of attractions—climate, fishing, boating, gambling, and folks trying to escape from whatever it is they keep trying to escape from. Lately, local booster groups have been making all sorts of rash predictions, like: "This area will become the tourist capital of the 21st century." Rash? Maybe. But given the mix we just mentioned, don't count 'em out!

Six miles north of Bullhead City is a major resort—Katherine Landing—with launching ramp, marina, motel, restaurant, and RV/camping facilities. It's operated under the auspices of the National Park Service, as are two other important shoreline facilities. One is Willow Beach, reachable off U.S. Route 93 en route to Hoover Dam. The other is Cottonwood Cove, which you can get to via a side road off U.S. Route 95, on the Nevada side of the river. You can rent a houseboat—an increasingly popular way of enjoying both Mohave and Mead—at Katherine Landing or Cottonwood Cove. North of Bullhead City you can catch State Route 68, which takes you to Kingman.

(Above) The Colorado River at Topock is the starting point for unique canoe trips through the Havasu National Wildlife Refuge, where the bird life, scenery, and fishing keep outdoor lovers returning time after time.
Dick Dietrich photo

(Right) Narrow 67-mile-long Lake Mohave winds through rugged canyons near Willow Beach.
J. Peter Mortimer photo

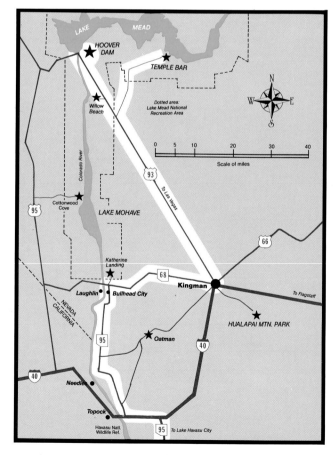

An alternate route to Kingman is via the original U.S. Route 66 (it's on your map but not numbered) through Oatman. This is an oft-patched bit of highway, so take it slow and easy. Oatman was a famous gold mining town which, as recently as pre-Depression days, had a population of more than 12,000. There was even a stock exchange there! Not much is left, but tourists like to stop by, if for no other reason than to see the burros. They're feral donkeys that forage in the desert, and they come into town and stroll down the main street as casually as if they owned the place.

Two miles east of Oatman, on the slopes west of Sitgreaves Pass, is all that remains of Goldroad, Oatman's gold-mining neighbor. It had its boom in the early part of the century. The hills thereabouts are laced with town foundations and mine shafts.

Several things give Kingman notability. It's a county seat. It's the town that Arizonans go through to get to Las Vegas. It's a stopover on the interstate. And it's the place where Andy Devine was born. Ah, child, who was Andy Devine, you ask? A movie star, is what he was, playing mostly support roles, with a voice as gravelly as a country road. He died in 1977, and there's an Andy Devine Room with personal memorabilia at the Mohave Museum of History and Arts, located at 400 West Beale Street.

There's also an exhibit of carved turquoise at the museum that's worth seeing. Kingman enjoyed a turquoise boom in the 1970s, with dealers coming from all over the world to buy a particularly high quality of turquoise mined in nearby Mineral Park.

Admission to the museum is free, but a donation is requested.

Fifteen miles southeastward is a kind of high-rise oasis, Hualapai Mountain Park, a county park slated to become part of the state park system. Dominating the scene is 8266-foot Hualapai Peak, tallest in this part of the state. Among the pines are campsites and picnic tables, cabins, and a lodge offering rooms and meals.

U.S. Route 93 takes you northwest out of Kingman to the next—and by far the larger—of the two big lakes that make up the Lake Mead National Recreation Area. It is, of course, Lake Mead itself. Mead is 105 miles long compared to Mohave's 67 miles.

Where you go from here depends on what you want to see. Want a good lakeshore view of the Arizona side? About 55 miles northwest of Kingman pick up a paved two-lane road which takes you to a place called Temple Bar on the south shore of Lake Mead, 30 miles or so from the main highway. It has just about everything you could want for a lake outing—boat rentals, lodging, restaurant, campground, and an upstream shoreline that even extends into the Grand Canyon!

Want to see Hoover Dam? Just stay on U.S. Route 93, which crosses it. You can stop there, tour the interior of the dam, view the monster turbines and look at the immense sweep of concrete which is the dam's downstream side.

(Opposite page) Named one of the seven modern civil engineering wonders of the United States, Hoover Dam has been toured by more than 22 million visitors since its completion in 1935. The 700-foot-high dam holds back the water of Lake Mead, the largest artificial body of water in the United States.
Alan Benoit photo

(Above) Houseboating on lakes Mead and Mohave has become a popular vacation adventure for many. Endless hours of leisurely cruising through dynamic desert scenery, sunning on idyllic white-sand beaches and swimming in cool emerald waters—all can be done with this sturdy craft that has all the conveniences of home.
Alan Benoit photo

**MONTEZUMA CASTLE •
OAK CREEK •
TUZIGOOT • JEROME**

Verde Valley • Sedona • Prescott

History and prehistory are just about everywhere you look in this state, which was, until fairly recently, a part of the Western frontier. And this tour really packs it in. Territorial capital...tumble-down mining camp... military fort dating back to the Indian wars...ancient ruins...these are some of the romantic ingredients of Tour 6.

Northbound on Interstate 17 from Phoenix, about 50 miles out, there's a special rest stop which is worth a few minutes. It's called Sunset Point. *Sunset* magazine (no connection) described it as the "ultimate in rest stops." It won first place in a Federal Highway Administration national rest stop competition in which there were entries from 28 states. It's equipped not only with the usual facilities, but also with ramadas, picnic tables, photo displays, and maps. It sits on a promontory that gives you a stirring view. You can take in the Bradshaw Mountains, part of Horsethief Basin, the site of a ghost town with the name of Bumblebee, and an old stagecoach trail.

One age of man peers over the shoulder of another in the Verde Valley. Tuzigoot, its roots lost in the dim past, was a forgotten ruin four centuries before the first pick tore into the mother lode of copper in Cleopatra Hill on which the city of Jerome, background, perches.
David Muench photo

Back on the road and another dozen miles north to Cordes Junction, you might like to leave the interstate long enough to take a look at Arcosanti. About a mile north of Cordes Junction on a dirt road, it is noted for futuristic design. Paolo Soleri, a world-renowned architect, urban planner, philosopher, and ex-protégé of Frank Lloyd Wright, conceived Arcosanti as an answer to urban sprawl and energy waste. When finished, which may be awhile, it's to be a vertical city rising some 25 stories and housing 4 or 5 thousand people. It's intended to be antisprawl (occupying only 14 acres of an 860-acre land parcel) and energy-efficient (solar for both heating and cooling).

The name Arcosanti is a marriage of "arcology" and "Cosanti," "arcology" being a marriage of "architecture" and "ecology," and "cosanti" an Italian word meaning "before things." (Cosanti is also the name of Soleri's studio in Scottsdale, which is included in Tour 9.) Soleri's architectural students provide the labor and pay for the privilege (a chance to study with the master). You can see the place for a nominal donation (there are hourly tours) and buy lunch there. Along about September of each year there's a big fall equinox festival at Arcosanti that attracts thousands.

Back again to I-17. Twenty-four miles farther, at the end of a downgrade that gives you a thrilling view of the Verde Valley, take the Camp Verde exit. Fort Verde was a cavalry outpost during the Indian wars of the late 19th century, a major base for General George Crook's forces protecting settlers from Apaches. On the porch of one of the four buildings now comprising the 10-acre Fort Verde State Historic Park, General Crook accepted the surrender of Apache chief Cha-lipun and 300 of his wariors. In the Fort Verde museum you'll find old military uniforms, rifles, and carbines, saddles, spurs, a field medical kit, Indian relics, some correspondence of the period and, of all things, a frontier wedding dress. There's a small admission charge.

Take Montezuma Castle north out of Camp Verde for five miles and you're at Montezuma Castle National Monument. It's not really a castle and has nothing to do with the Aztec rulers who bore the name Montezuma. What can be said for it, though, is that it's one of the more magnificent of all the West's prehistoric cliff dwellings. It's five stories tall, tucked away in a recess high in a great limestone cliff above Beaver Creek. The occupants were probably the same Sinagua who occupied Wupatki and Walnut Canyon (see Tour 3).

Go back to I-17, drive four miles farther north, then leave the interstate at McGuireville, and drive four more miles toward Rimrock. You'll come across another part of the same national monument. This one is called Montezuma Well. But just as the castle isn't a castle, this isn't a well. It's a big limestone sink with more cliff dwellings lining the crater walls above the water. The aboriginals who lived in the area diverted water from the sink into ditches to irrigate their farmland below.

There's an admission charge at Montezuma Castle but not at Montezuma Well.

Retrace your steps to McGuireville, go another five miles north, and take the turnoff (State Route 179) to

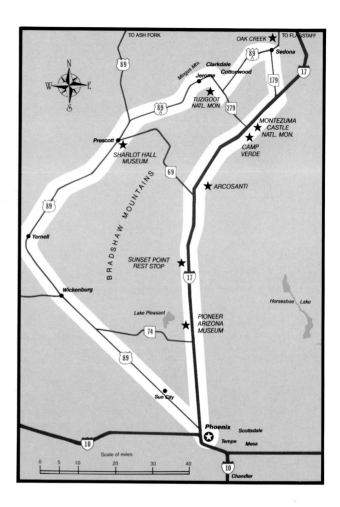

Sedona, Oak Creek Canyon, and Red Rock Country. The rocks include huge red sandstone monoliths, and the region is one of those perfect parts of the state—gorgeous scenery and great year-round weather—that keeps drawing people back again and again. The population in 1970 was only 2000. Then Sedona got *discovered*, and at this writing it has over 10,000 year-round residents, about half of them retirees. Land values have skyrocketed, and everybody who moves in wishes they could close the gate behind them.

What to see? Well, Tlaquepaque, for one thing, pronounced t'lah-kay-*pah*-kay. It is named after an artsy suburb of Guadalajara, Mexico, and comprises as unique a collection of art galleries and craft shops—and, yes, restaurants—as you're likely to find. The builders set out to replicate a colonial Mexican village and accomplished just that. The bell tower at Tlaquepaque is a Sedona landmark.

There are numerous excellent galleries around town—Sedona goes in big for art. But it goes in for other things, too, like wearing out the seat of your blue jeans slithering down Slide Rock, which is a natural water chute in Oak Creek just above Sedona. Swimmers (usually wearing old denims instead of swim togs because they *do* wear out the seats of their pants) are jet-propelled down the slide and dumped into a natural pool. Real neat in hot weather.

Oak Creek Canyon is a great gash in the mountains. U.S. Route 89-A winds its way up the canyon toward Flagstaff. It is the setting for Zane Grey's novel, *Call of the Canyon*. It's also summer resort country, with all manner of rustic retreats, and one of the prime places in the state to look for fall color when the mercury starts dropping.

You might figure on spending the night at Sedona. There are nice motels and lodges in and around the town.

From Sedona, take U.S. Route 89-A southwestward to Cottonwood, a comfortable little town which—like just about every other place in the Verde Valley—is growing briskly. (You'll need to leave U.S. Route 89-A momentarily and take the business route into Cottonwood.) Across the Verde River from downtown Cottonwood is Dead Horse Ranch State Park, which is noted for bird-watching, river-watching, and just sort of sitting for a spell. (There are campsites, with electric and sewer hookups for RVs.)

Between Cottonwood and its neighbor, Clarkdale, there's a turnoff to still another prehistoric Indian ruin, which is also a national monument. This one is called Tuzigoot. It's a pueblo of a hundred or so rooms built by the Sinagua during the 13th century, when they came south. The ruins lay forgotten and ignored for centuries. Then, in the 1930s, archeologists from the University of Arizona went to work excavating and restoring them. The pueblo rests on a 120-foot-high ridge from which you get a

The Sinagua people, Pueblo Indian farmers, built Montezuma Castle high in a limestone cliff recess during the 12th century. The magnificent 20-room, five-story structure is partially excavated. Lower rooms are open to visitors today, and artifacts are on display in the monument's nearby visitors center.
Jerry Jacka photo

striking view of the Verde Valley. There are trail walks, a museum with exhibits, and an admission charge.

Clarkdale, the next town as you move northwestward (you're still on that same business route), was—for a lot

Verde Valley • Sedona • Prescott   47

(Top) On the porch of the Fort Verde commanding officer's quarters, Apache Chief Cha-lipun surrendered to General George Crook, admitting there were "too many cartridges of copper." Jerry Jacka photo

(Above) Slide Rock is a refreshing stop for Oak Creek Canyon visitors. Bob Bradshaw photo

(Right) The awesome beauty of Oak Creek Canyon owes its sudden changes in vegetation and rock formations to a dramatic drop in altitude. Large sculptured spires are surrounded by hundreds of other sandstone bastions which have resisted wind and water while, through eons of time, the softer material around them has been carried off. David Muench

of years—the smelter half of the Jerome-Clarkdale copper-producing axis. The copper came out of the mines at Jerome, on the nearby mountainside, and was carted down the hill to the Clarkdale smelters. The local landmark was one of the tallest unsupported masonry smokestacks in the world. 'Tis said hereabouts that the engineer who built it learned that a similar stack somewhere else was going to be five feet higher. So he added 25 feet, and the Clarkdale stack rose to more than 400 feet.

When Jerome's mines closed in 1951, Clarkdale just about folded up. But it had a timely revival when a cement company came in during the 1950s. Much of its product went north in trucks leaving every half-hour around the clock for the Colorado River dam then abuilding at Glen Canyon.

Rejoin U.S. Route 89-A on the other side of Clarkdale and head up Cleopatra Hill to Jerome, three miles west. It's a gutsy little ghost town with a lot of live ghosts. Once upon a time there were 15,000 people in Jerome, and a New York newspaper called it the "wickedest town in the West." When the mines closed, only a few people stayed around. But then folks began drifting back, along about the 1960s, and today Jerome has a population of several hundred. They're mainly retirees, artists, and people who like the quiet life . . . and also the view, which is a knockout. In the near distance are Sedona's scrumptious red rocks and beyond them can be seen Flagstaff's San Francisco Peaks.

The signs of yesteryear that you find in this precarious old mining camp include buckled sidewalks, abandoned houses teetering on their ancient stilts above switchback streets, and a jail that slid across the street and came to rest in a vacant lot. Someone posted a sign on it—not inappropriate, really: "Keep Out."

But there has been a lot of restoration, too. The mansion of James S. (Rawhide Jimmy) Douglas, who dug one of Jerome's main mines and prospered greatly therefrom, has become the Jerome State Historic Park. Here all manner of things are on exhibit to show you what Jerome was like in its heyday. There's a mine museum downtown where you can imagine how copper was mined underground nearly a century ago. (Admission charge to both.) Jerome today retains many quaint craft shops and antique stores—even one "junktique" emporium. And a turn-of-the-century bordello is now a restaurant.

Verde Valley • Sedona • Prescott 49

If you stay on U.S. Route 89-A as it goes through Jerome and over Mingus Mountain (elevation 7743 feet), you'll reach the junction with U.S. Route 89 about 25 miles to the southwest and five miles from there the city of Prescott. There's a lot of early Western flavor here, too, and it starts right in the middle of town with a fine, robust old stone courthouse, in front of which stands a classic equestrian statue. The rider by popular myth is Buckey O'Neill, a man of astonishing versatility — soldier, adventurer, poet, scholar, editor, judge, sheriff, and mayor. He died in the fighting at San Juan Hill, Cuba, in the Spanish-American War. The statue was done by Solon Borglum, whose brother, Gutzon, carved the heads on Mount Rushmore.

Across the street is Whiskey Row (more properly, a block of Montezuma Street). In the old days it had so many saloons that it was, for all practical purposes, just one long bar. (In point of fact, Prescott's first saloon was located some distance from Montezuma Street, on the bank of Granite Creek. But the location was bad for business. As one old-timer was later heard to explain, "The sight of water made the customers sick.")

Three blocks west of the courthouse on Gurley Street is a tidy little enclave of Arizona history. Prescott, it needs

(Left) Almost a ghost town after the mines closed, the one-time copper camp of Jerome has come back to life. Today, more than 700,000 tourists each year are attracted to this enchanting town. Dick Dietrich photo

(Above) Jerome's mines made history — to the tune of $42 million — under James S. "Rawhide Jimmy" Douglas. His home, now Jerome State Historic Park, stands proudly atop a knoll near the old mine.

Thomas Ives photo

to be remembered, was the capital of Arizona Territory for two different periods. The enclave is known as the Sharlot Hall Museum. Sharlot Hall was a pioneer poet and historian who collected many of the early exhibits found therein. Clustered hereabouts are about a dozen buildings, including the Governor's Mansion, built of logs in 1864. It housed not only the governor but the territorial legislature, since the members thereof found the building warmer than the one in which they were supposed to meet. Another log building is one of Prescott's first boarding houses. The frontiersmen good-naturedly alluded to it as Fort Misery, and the name stuck.

Gathered at the museum are historic documents, newspapers dating back to the 1860s, fine Indian artifacts, and thousands of historic photos, including famous glass plates depicting the surrender of the Apache chief Geronimo. Sharlot Hall Museum also features special exhibits on specific aspects of Southwest history.

The museum's archives are housed in a recently built solar-heated museum center. There's no admission fee to the Sharlot Hall Museum.

Across town, at Arizona Avenue and Willis Street, is the Smoki Museum, a collection of Indian objects created by the Smoki People of Prescott. They're a group of business and professional people who put on Indian dances (including a simulation of the famous snake dance of the Hopis) every August. The museum is open June 1 to September 1 and donations are accepted. Prescott also has some delightful scenic attractions, Granite Dells and Lynx Lake to mention just a couple, and there are good accommodations in Prescott should you decide to spend the night.

Pick up U.S. Route 89 again and follow it southwestward another 59 miles to Wickenburg. En route you'll come out of the high pine country to a jumping-off place called Yarnell Hill that gives you an extraordinary view

(Top, left) In Granite Dells, just north of Prescott, lies Watson Lake. Centuries of erosion left the steep granite walls topped with figures resembling human and animal forms in hues of pink, gray, brown, and red.
Dick Dietrich photo

(Right) The C.A. Sewall House, completed in 1893, is only one of many beautiful New England style homes built by Easterners during Prescott's early days. During the territorial period Prescott served as the capital; it remains the Yavapai County seat.
Kathleen Norris Cook photo

(Bottom, left) An all-American good time draws a crowd to down-town Prescott. Each Fourth of July weekend the town celebrates Frontier Days where local citizens, plus visitors from all over Arizona, turn out for the parade, fireworks, and the world's oldest rodeo.
Thomas Ives photo

of the desert floor and rugged horizons below.

More than a century old, Wickenburg is a gold-mining and cattle town within view of the southern tip of the Bradshaws (Prescott being in the northern portion). It was named after a Prussian prospector, one Henry Wickenburg, who, legend has it, threw a rock at a cranky mule only to see the rock crack open and reveal gold. Result: the opening of nearby Vulture Mine, one of Arizona's richest, and the founding of a town which—though its gold rush is long gone—has managed to look more Western than most western towns. You encounter signs like "Keep Your Horse Off the Sidewalk" (that's not altogether in jest—there are dude ranches and working ranches all around) and, at the Hassayampa River crossing, "No Fishing From the Bridge." Big deal. There's almost never any water in the river anyway. Good thing. By legend, he who drinks from the Hassayampa never tells the truth again.

Stroll up Frontier Street, which, with its overhanging roofs and hitching posts, looks like something left over from the early 1900s. Drop in at the Desert Caballeros Western Museum (there's an admission charge) for a peek at some of the rustic gadgets that the old miners and prospectors used. And out behind the town hall is Old 761, a Santa Fe steam locomotive that used to puff back and forth between the West and Chicago.

Then there's the old jail tree at the corner of Tegner and Center. It dates back to the days when Wickenburg couldn't afford a jail. Miscreants were chained to this venerable mesquite, and on Sundays their families would come bearing picnic goodies.

You go back to Phoenix on U.S. Route 60-89, perhaps stopping en route for a look-see at the largest and snazziest of this nation's retirement communities—Sun City. Population: about 60,000. Bear in mind that it was just farmland some 25 years ago.

Verde Valley • Sedona • Prescott 53

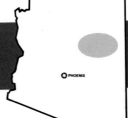

PHOENIX

Mogollon Rim • Petrified Forest

Slicing northwest-southeast through this rugged central-to-eastern part of Arizona is a gigantic geological feature known as the Mogollon Rim (pronounced, in these parts, *muggy-own*). It's Arizona's dropping-off place—a mighty escarpment of rock and timber, rising, in places, to a height greater than 8000 feet. It extends nearly 300 miles, all the way into New Mexico, and separates the lofty plateau country of the north from the low country to the south. Some call it Tonto Rim.

Zane Grey, the author, liked that name best, and he loved the country. He hunted and fished here. He built a cabin in the shadow of the rim, and it was there that he wrote some of his more famous novels, even basing them on the shoot-from-the-hip history of the area. One was *Under the Tonto Rim*. Another was *To the Last Man*, a fictional reenactment of a classic cattle-sheep war in nearby Pleasant Valley.

For the traveler eager to explore, Zane Grey's Tonto Rim Country is alive with adventures at every turn. Aside from fabulous scenery there are reminders everywhere of this land's rich and colorful past.
Dick Dietrich photo

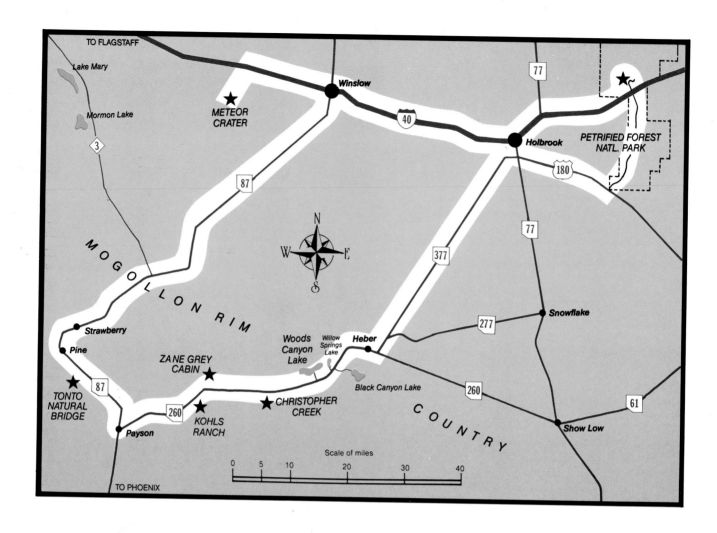

For convenience, you might start at Payson, which is by way of being the capital of Zane Grey Country. (If you're starting from Phoenix, allow about two hours for the 90 miles to Payson. State Route 87 is good, but twisty when it gets into the mountains.)

Payson is a mix of cow town, lumber town, and resort town with a population of about 6000. It was named after a man who never saw it—U.S. Senator Louis E. Payson of Illinois. He was responsible for the appointment of Payson's first postmaster, Frank Hise. So Hise reciprocated by naming the town after Payson.

Head on north on State Route 87 which, about a dozen miles later, brings you to the turnoff to Tonto Natural Bridge. It's the largest natural travertine bridge in the world, rising 183 feet above the silvery waters of Pine Creek. Its length is 400 feet. There used to be, in fact, an entire farm on top of it. Formed by limestone deposits from mineral springs flowing out of an adjacent mountain, the bridge is so large that people right alongside it sometimes don't see it. You have to reach a certain vantage point to look down into the canyon. The bridge is privately owned and there's an admission fee. There's also a lodge dating to the 1920s.

Back to the main highway and on northward a few miles into Pine, which rests just below the edge of the

(Right, top) Thanks to flowing springs, Tonto Natural Bridge is a living and constantly changing sculpture. Stalagmites and stalactites grow at the rate of one and a half inches each year.
Thomas Ives photo

(Right) One of the West's most unusual wonders is Meteor Crater. It is about 20 miles west of Winslow, and just a few minutes' side trip off Interstate 40.
Collier-Condit photo

Mogollon Rim. It was settled about a century ago by the Church of Jesus Christ of Latter-day Saints (Mormons) migrating from Utah. Three miles farther and you're at Strawberry. It's noted mainly, as is much of the rest of the Rim country, as a weekend cooling off place for Phoenix residents trying to avoid the summer heat. Visit the Strawberry schoolhouse, restored.

Then up and over the Rim, a quiet, woodsy drive that takes you finally out of the high pines and deposits you on the Colorado plateau. It's a bit under 70 miles from Strawberry to Winslow, which sits in the valley of the Little Colorado River and is noted for (1) what it used to be and (2) the many interesting places you can get to from here.

What it used to be was one of the grandest railroad towns in the West. It was — still is, in fact — on the main line of the Santa Fe. Winslow these days is making a special effort to entertain and inform travelers with a new visitors center along Interstate 40.

Winslow serves as point of departure for sight-seeing the Navajo and Hopi Indian reservations to the north; the Rim country, of course, to the south; and Meteor Crater to the west. First, head for Meteor Crater.

Eighteen miles west of Winslow on Interstate 40 and then six miles south on a paved road you reach this remarkable celestial calling card. Scientists date the crater about 22,000 years before the present and say it was caused by an enormous meteor plunging out of space at a speed of 33,000 miles per hour. When it hit, it destroyed all plant and animal life within 100 miles. It dug a hole 570 feet deep (deeper than the Washington Monument is high), 4150 feet across, and more than three miles in circumference.

The crater was discovered in 1871 and has been used by the National Aeronautics and Space Administration to train astronauts for their walks on the moon. There's a museum with exhibits and souvenirs. The whole layout, crater included, is privately owned, and there's an admission charge.

Back, then, to Winslow and eastward on I-40 through Joseph City (said to be the oldest Mormon settlement in Arizona) to Holbrook. You'll go a long way to find a town with a more sanguine past than Holbrook. It was here, about a hundred years ago, that Sheriff Commodore Perry Owens (his title was sheriff; his name was Commodore) killed three men and wounded a fourth in a shoot-out related to the same Pleasant Valley cattle-sheep war that so intrigued Zane Grey. It was here also that a local sheriff got chewed out by no less a dignitary than the President of the United States for issuing invitations to a hanging in which he promised: "The latest improved methods in the art of scientific strangulation will be employed and everything possible will be done to make the surroundings cheerful and the execution a success."

You might plan to spend the night in Holbrook. No hangings are likely to take place, and there are a number of good motels.

Then, next day, on to the north entrance to the Painted Desert and Petrified Forest National Park, 26 miles east of Holbrook. Tarry awhile at the Painted Desert Visitors Center so you can soak up some information about what

(Above) In 1895 local rancher Adam Hanna called it Chalcedony Park, that curious area of "stone trees" in northeastern Arizona now known as Petrified Forest National Park. Even back then it was a favorite of tourists. David Muench photo

(Right) The Painted Desert broods or smiles depending on the weather. Its color comes from irregularly eroded beds of sediment and bentonite clay. The desert, in its 200-mile stretch across northern Arizona, embraces Petrified Forest National Park.

Kaz Hagiwara photo

(Right) Christopher Creek campground, 24 miles east of Payson, is a perfect resting place after a full day exploring the Mogollon Rim Country.
P. K. Weis photo

(Far right) Dawn on Woods Canyon Lake. This picturesque man-made reservoir in the tall pines is an ideal spot to fish, camp, or just relax.
David Muench photo

it is you're going to see. There's a 17-minute film about how the wood became petrified. The show is worth watching, and you'll almost surely be startled, as so many folks are, when you realize how close we came to losing the Petrified Forest.

It wasn't even discovered until the mid-1800s, and then people began ransacking it for souvenirs, gemstones, and petrified logs to take on exhibition. Finally, in 1906, after numerous appeals from citizens of what was then the Territory of Arizona, President Theodore Roosevelt set the area aside as a national monument. But not until 1962, after Arizonan Stewart Udall became Secretary of the Interior, did the Petrified Forest become a national park. These days the Park Service is understandably picky about folks taking any of the petrified wood with them. (Your car may be checked before you leave. Thieves may be prosecuted.)

The park road takes you in a lazy loop through the Painted Desert. There are several lookouts and observation sites. At Kachina Point is located the venerable Painted

Desert Inn. It was built in 1924 and is now on the National Register of Historic Places. Kachina Point is also a good place to take pictures of the Painted Desert. Best times are at sunrise and sunset when the red hues of the sun bring out the multicolored magnificence of the landscape.

You'll re-cross I-40 heading south and stop at places like Puerco Ruin (occupied by prehistoric peoples as early as A.D. 300) and Newspaper Rock (where aboriginals carved out petroglyphs still being studied by scientists for clues to their civilization). On southward, then, for varying glimpses of petrified logs at places like Jasper Forest, Crystal Forest, and Blue Mesa (where you can also take a very interesting closed-loop hike). The main road through the park is 28 miles long. If you take the available side roads to points of interest, you'll be driving some 38 miles in all. And do, please, get out of the car now and again to hike some of the trails and get close-up looks at the petrified wood. Let your imagination play with the notion of what happened 200 million years ago when giant creatures half as big as a freight car roamed this land

and tall pine-like trees grew on distant hills. When the trees fell they were carried onto the flood plain and buried under tons of mud, silt, and volcanic ash. These deposits blocked out oxygen and smothered the decaying action that normally would have taken place. Water-borne chemicals, such as silica, replaced the wood fibers and turned the logs to stone.

The last major stop at the south end of the park is the Rainbow Forest Museum, which has a service station and gift shop. You emerge onto U.S. Route 180 and take a right turn to Holbrook, 17 miles away, then south on State Route 377 to return to Zane Grey Country. You go through Heber (having merged with State Route 277 and State Route 260). Just where State Route 260 begins its descent of the Rim, a paved Forest Service road jogs north, then goes along the edge of the Rim. You will find—if you can take the time for this slight detour—a little gem of a lake. It's Woods Canyon Lake, set in the center of a large recreation area. Quiet (no motor boats), green, and cool.

Now, as you start back down the Mogollon Rim, you see the vast ponderosa pine region. Stop at one or two of the viewpoints for a long, slow look at that magnificent land mass which Zane Grey described rapturously as "a split, tossed, dimpled, heaving, rolling world of black-green forestland."

This is choice hunting and fishing country. Cabins are hidden back among the trees on both sides of the road as you cruise toward Payson, and there are accommodations at places like Christopher Creek and Kohls Ranch. A Forest Service road north of Kohls Ranch takes you to Zane Grey's cabin five miles from the highway, near the headwaters of Tonto Creek. The cabin is open to the public from March 1 to November 30 (there's an admission fee) and it contains Grey's writing board, the original manuscript of *Under the Tonto Rim*, guns that Grey hunted with, photographs, and other memorabilia.

The road over the Rim from Heber to Payson is 54 miles, and Payson has some good motels if you want to put down for the night.

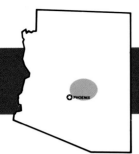
Apache Trail • Mining Towns

This tour takes in one of the more dramatic scenic regions of the state, with a bit of lusty history thrown in for good measure. And it offers the added advantage of being close to the Phoenix metropolitan area.

Pick up U.S. Route 60-89 as it heads east out of Phoenix, via East Van Buren Street, through Tempe and Mesa. It becomes Apache Boulevard as you round the bend in Tempe where Arizona State University showcases its Frank Lloyd Wright-designed Gammage Center for the Performing Arts.

In Mesa you might like to pause at the Mormon Temple, 525 East Main, an architectural attraction in its own right. The majestic edifice, which serves the Church of Jesus Christ of Latter-day Saints throughout the Southwest, is open only to Mormons. There is a visitors center, however, with the welcome mat out for non-Mormons. The center contains two theaters showing church-related films, and there are tours every half-hour. The grounds of the temple are manicured, and the gardens are stunningly beautiful year-round.

Then on eastward 15 miles to Apache Junction and northeastward onto the Apache Trail (it's State Route 88 on your map). What makes this road so very special is its scenic grandeur — massive buttes, prickly desert, twisting canyons, lovely lakes, and, hovering over much of it, the spectral, glowering, volcanic dome known as the Superstition Mountains.

A small warning: the road is paved for only the first 20 miles. Beyond that, gravel, until you reach Roosevelt Lake.

But don't let that deter you from taking this thrilling trip through what President Theodore Roosevelt (the lake was named for him) described as "the most awe-inspiring and most sublimely beautiful panorama Nature has ever created." The trail, in fact, was hacked through the wilderness to move supplies and equipment into the mountains for the building, 1906-1911, of Roosevelt Dam, the largest masonry dam in the world. The dam and lake comprised the first major development under the Reclamation Act

(Above) The Arizona Temple of the Church of Jesus Christ of Latter-day Saints in Mesa not only serves as a religious center for Mormons but is a tourist attraction as well. The visitors center is open to the public.
Dick Dietrich photo

(Right) Of the numerous legends associated with the Superstition Mountains one of the most appealing is the Pima Indian myth which ascribes a tawny colored band of rock near the top of a portion of the mountain to the high water mark of the Great Flood.
Jerry Jacka photo

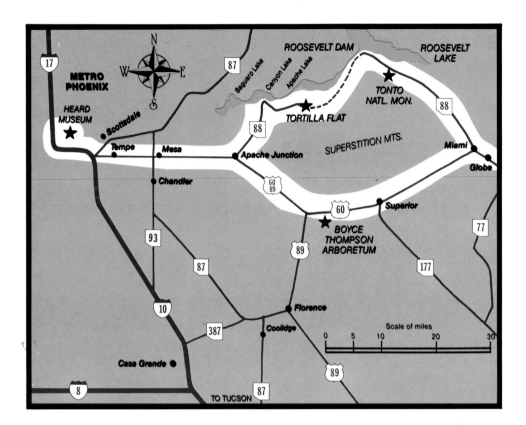

of 1902. Roosevelt Dam is the keystone of the Salt River Project, which transformed Phoenix and its environs into an enormous desert oasis. The Apache Trail skirts three of the four lakes which descend the mountains toward the valley.

Five miles from Apache Junction there's a turnoff into Lost Dutchman State Park, on the slopes of the storied Superstition Mountains. The park is a 300-acre expanse of desert named for a German prospector, Jacob Walz, known as the "Dutchman," who—or so goes the apocryphal tale—found a gold mine in the Superstitions. Then he was so inconsiderate as to die before he would tell anybody its whereabouts. The Lost Dutchman is one of the more celebrated "lost mines" in the West. Maps purporting to reveal its whereabouts keep showing up, usually handed down by grandfathers who got them from uncles who got them from prospectors who got them from the Dutchman himself. And so people still hunt for the mine, and some of them have been killed for their trouble.

You go through Goldfield, a ghost town with still-visible ruins of its old gold-rush days. Then starts the head-turning scenery that makes the Apache Trail so distinctive—tumbled volcanic debris, bronze-walled cliffs, saguaro-strewn mountain slopes. In addition to the Superstitions there are two mountain masses along the trail—the Mazatzals and the Sierra Anchas. Desert or no, they often wear snow caps after a winter storm.

Canyon Lake, a dozen or so miles east of Apache Junction, is the first of the three that lie along the trail. Like the others, Canyon Lake not only stores irrigation water but serves as a recreational mecca—boating, water-

skiing, fishing, whatever. You can rent boats at all the lakes.

East of Canyon Lake you reach Tortilla Flat, a small motel, restaurant, store, and Forest Service campground. There are interesting outcroppings of rock thereabouts. Five miles beyond Tortilla Flat the pavement ends. Then comes the real excitement of the Apache Trail—Fish Creek Hill. It's a scary plunge into Fish Creek Canyon on a road so narrow that cars turn out to let other cars pass. But one of the advantages of traveling the trail eastward instead of westward is that you go *down* Fish Creek Hill instead of up, and can see cars approaching from a distance. Also you're hugging the canyon wall as you descend. For these reasons, and because people are extremely careful on Fish Creek Hill, accidents are rare.

The road arrives at Apache Lake, which many Apache Trail *aficionados* like best. It's less frequented, and the view of the lake from the road, as you turn off to head down a steep descent toward the water's edge, is simply breathtaking.

Beyond Apache Lake you pass Roosevelt Dam and then its lake. It's a big mushroom-shaped body of water spreading east and north along the Sierra Anchas. It's bass fishing heaven.

The road is paved once again, and three miles past Roosevelt Lake you will find the turnoff to Tonto National Monument, a particularly well-preserved complex of cliff dwellings occupied by the Salado Indians well over half a millenium ago. There's a museum with dioramas, artifacts, and samples of Salado weaving, weapons, tools, and jewelry. There are three sets of ruins—upper with 40 rooms, lower with 20 rooms, and the lower ruin annex with 12 rooms. Getting to the upper ruin takes a bit of

doing and special arrangements with the rangers, but the rest are easily accessible. There's the usual charge for admission.

Then on to Globe/Miami, twin mining towns that constitute the eastern anchor of the Apache Trail. These communities provide accommodations, should you suddenly find that you've spent more time enjoying the scenery than you'd realized.

Silver gave Globe its start (according to legend, the town got its name from a 50-pound globe-shaped nugget of nearly pure silver). Today the mining is mainly in and around Miami, and it's almost all copper. You have no trouble telling that it's a mining town. Part of the 160 million tons of tailings (that's earthen debris with the minerals removed) crowd the roadway. Back in copper's halcyon days the Inspiration Consolidated Copper Co. conducted daily tours of the open pit, smelter, and other facilities. The tours were discontinued with copper's cutbacks, but en route through Miami you might take a moment to phone the company's headquarters and see if they're on again.

Near Globe lies another Salado Indian ruin, not as well-preserved as Tonto but more extensive. Located a mile south of town on the Pinal Mountain Road, it covers about two acres and is called *Besh-ba-Gowah*, an Apache word meaning "metal camp." The Globe Community Center, with its developed picnic area, is also located here. Artifacts from Besh-ba-Gowah are housed in the Gila County Historical Museum, back along the highway.

Then head west on U.S. Route 60. It's much faster and smoother than the Apache Trail but has its own brand of scenic charisma, particularly as you cruise down Queen

(Above) Roosevelt Dam irrigates the Salt River Valley and helps Phoenix remain a green oasis in the desert. The dam on the Salt River reaches 284 feet in height and is *184 feet thick at the base. Its creation was supervised by the Bureau of Reclamation. Capacity of the power plant at the base is 24,000 horsepower.*
Earl Petroff photo

At Tonto National Monument visitors catch a glimpse of what life was like along the bank of the Salt River in the 14th century. Within the 1120-acre monument two major cliff dwellings have been preserved. The photo shows Upper Ruin, left, Lower Ruin, right, and the visitors center. Pottery, stone work, fragments of clothing, beans, squash, nuts, and small ears of corn, displayed in the visitors center, bring the culture to life.
Jerry Jacka photo

(Inset) The dwellings have been so well protected, in their cliff-face niche, that touring parties can see some of the original roof timbers as well as finger marks in the wall plaster.
Jeff Gnass photo

Creek Canyon and through the Queen Creek tunnel to the town of Superior, at the foot of the mountains. The Magma Copper Company mine at Superior is said to be one of the 25 deepest in the world.

A short distance past Superior you can take a side road to the Apache Tears Mine. Apache tears are glassy nodules of volcanic obsidian. Legend has it the United States Cavalry trapped a band of Apaches on a height overlooking Superior. Rather than surrender, the Indians leaped to their deaths. And, so the tale goes, the wives of the dead warriors mourned for many days. Apache gods turned their tears into beautiful black, glossy stones. You'll want to take that story with a grain of obsidian, but for a modest sum you can dig up some Apache tears for yourself. Or buy some polished ones.

Three miles west of Superior is the Boyce Thompson Southwestern Arboretum. Thousands of species of desert plants from all over the world, plus birds and animals, are on exhibit, and there's important plant research going on. The founder was mining magnate William Boyce Thompson. On a Red Cross mercy mission to Russia in 1917 he saw so much hunger and misery that he decided there was nothing quite so important as research into living plants for food, clothing and shelter. The arboretum and a sister research institution at Cornell University resulted. The arboretum operates as a field museum of the University of Arizona. There's an admission fee.

An arboretum bonus is the one-and-a-quarter-mile Picket Post Trail that loops away from the main display area and on through a craggy desert landscape. It's a

special kind of nature walk. Don't miss it if you can find the time. And do take in Thompson's rococo desert mansion, known as Picket Post House. Its 26 rooms, stacked atop a huge rock with a breathtaking view of Picket Post Mountain and nearby Queen Creek, are chockful of antiques and memorabilia that Thompson collected as he sailed his yacht to distant places. He copied the basic design of the mansion from a monastery he saw and admired in Greece and then, after the mansion was built, made impulsive changes. His daughter wanted to give a party and decided there wasn't enough room for her guests. So Thompson converted a patio into a large room. The Picket Post House has been authorized for addition to the state's park system.

En route to the metropolitan area, you might want to detour for a look at an interesting air museum. It's the Champlin Fighter Museum at Falcon Field east of Mesa. On exhibit are about 30 fighter planes from World War I and II (all or nearly all of them restored and ready to fly again). Also to be seen are more than 700 autographed photos of flying aces from 17 nations and all the wars through Vietnam, plus an array of World War II combat paintings. The museum bears the name of its founder, Douglas Champlin, a Mesa businessman fascinated by fighter planes and high performance machinery. It's also the headquarters of the American Fighter Aces Association. Directions: at the Bush Highway, about halfway between Apache Junction and Mesa, turn north. Go three miles to McKellips Road and then three miles west to Falcon Field. There's an admission charge.

Valley of the Sun · Phoenix

This may come as a surprise, but, truth to tell, there's no such place as the Valley of the Sun. That is to say, it doesn't show up on a map. It's not a geographically precise entity. Properly speaking, it is the Salt River Valley. But that doesn't sound very romantic. Valley of the Sun does. And people flooding into this area during the boom years following World War II adopted "Valley of the Sun" as part of their language. They spoke — and still speak — of living in the Valley of the Sun...of visitors coming out to the Valley of the Sun...of the future of the Valley of the Sun...and, of course, the media have done their share of perpetuating this benign bit of Chamber of Commerce fiction.

Anyway, what we have here *is* a valley, and a lovely one. And it does receive wondrous amounts of sunshine.

We're calling this a one- or two-day tour because, in terms of distance, it can be covered easily in a day but you may want to spend two days so as not to be rushed.

Let's start by driving up Interstate 17 to the Pioneer Arizona Living History Museum, 25 miles north of downtown Phoenix. It's quite what the name implies — a museum of living history. There aren't just relics and artifacts on display. There are whole buildings and complexes — a miners' camp, a gingerbread Victorian mansion, a school-

The modern skyline of downtown Phoenix still retains reminders of its Southwestern heritage: (left to right) the Hyatt Regency Hotel, the Valley Bank Center, and St. Mary's Church with its Spanish Colonial architecture. In a little over 100 years, Phoenix has grown from a hay camp of 100 pioneers to the ninth-largest city in the United States. Josef Muench photo

house and teacherage from the 1890s, an 1870 opera house, a stage station. Pioneer Arizona is a non-profit community enterprise. The schedule varies according to the season. Call 993-0212 for times.

Backtrack a couple of miles south on I-17 to pick up the Carefree Highway eastbound. Drive about 8 miles on this paved road until it intersects Cave Creek Road and turn left. It is also called Desert Foothills Drive because folks who cared greatly about the desert went to the trouble of making and installing 101 roadside markers identifying different species of desert plants native to the Sonoran Desert. Easy does it as you travel this bit of road. There are lots of dips. You'll enjoy learning the names of things that grow on the desert.

Cave Creek is the first of the two communities that you come to. It is an old rustic desert town with a dollop of authentic Western history. It was a mining camp in the 1880s and a ranching community when the mines played out. Phoenicians fleeing rampant growth have begun migrating out this way for some quieter living. Homes dot the desert and the cactus-covered hillsides.

Round the curve eastward a mile or so and you're in Carefree. It's a good deal fancier than Cave Creek, mainly because it was planned that way. Back in the 1950s a couple of real estate men spotted this princely piece of desert real estate located in a kind of bowl rimmed by mountains. They set about to make it a development of plush homes.

A realization of community priorities is unmistakable as you glimpse the street names: Long Rifle Road, Never Mind Trail, Nonchalant Avenue, Elbow Bend, Rocking Chair Road, and so forth.

A couple of interesting Carefree superlatives: in the center of the community, marking the location of a couple of attractive shopping areas, is the world's largest sundial (or maybe it's the second largest— there's some debate over that). And a few miles to the north is the world's largest Kachina doll, 50 feet tall, at a residential development called Tonto Hills.

Take Tom Darlington Drive (Scottsdale Road) southward out of Carefree. About halfway to Scottsdale you'll come upon Rawhide, one of the state's several built-from-

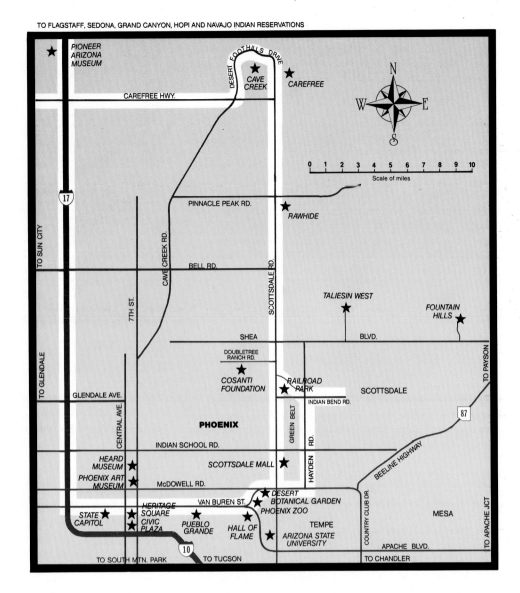

(Left) The Boulders Golf Course exemplifies the respect and land conciousness of developers in Carefree, northeast of Phoenix. Viewed from the road, the course is virtually indistinguishable from the surrounding desert, with greens recessed or hidden by gigantic boulders and golf cart paths dyed to match the desert floor.
Jerry Jacka photo

(Left, below) Rawhide, an authentic 1880s Western town re-created on 160 acres north of Scottsdale. The town attracts locals as well as tourists with its restaurant and saloon, shops, shoot-outs stagecoach rides, and wild west shows.
James Tallon photo

scratch Western towns to beguile the wandering tourist. It's also one of the better ones, with lots of frontier exotica — Geronimo's moccasins, Tom Mix's boots, Belle Starr's buffalo-horn table.

Just south of Bell Road, you'll cross the Granite Reef Aqueduct of the billion-dollar Central Arizona Project, built to bring Colorado River water over the mountains and across the desert into the valley and also to Tucson.

This particular locale, between Bell and Cactus roads, near Scottsdale Road, is the center of Arabian horse breeding and training in the United States. There are breeding farms all about. Arabian horse shows during the winter season have become a major Scottsdale attraction. If you're interested in visiting an Arabian ranch, you can call the Arabian Horse Association of Arizona for times and places.

The next major east-west thoroughfare south of Cactus Road is Shea Boulevard, which takes you eastward to two points of interest: Taliesin West and Fountain Hills. Taliesin (four miles east of Scottsdale Road and two miles north from the turnoff, which is marked) was built by Frank

Lloyd Wright. It is the winter headquarters of his famous architectural foundation.

Taliesin West is located on the western slopes of the McDowell Mountains; its startling redwood-and-rock design carries out the Wright philosophy of harmonizing architectural design with nature. Students come here from all over the world to learn and live in what is virtually a monastic environment. Tours are available (for a fee) between 10 a.m. and 4 p.m. daily from October to June, 9 to 10 a.m. from June to October.

Fountain Hills, on the other side of the McDowell Mountains, eight miles east of the Taliesin turnoff, was originally noted for its tallest fountain in the world (560 feet). But the place has grown into a self-contained community of considerable dimension. Not surprisingly, the idea of the fountain originated with the same master of massive gimmicks who brought you the London Bridge at Lake Havasu City, the late Robert McCulloch (see Tour 4). The fountain runs 10 minutes of every hour (on the hour). Environmentally interesting, the crystal clear plume is made from recycled sewer treatment water.

Valley of the Sun • Phoenix 71

Backtrack to Scottsdale Road, go south a mile, and turn west onto Double Tree Ranch Road to the Cosanti Foundation. This is the studio and planning center where architect and urban planner Paolo Soleri conceived his high-rise city now going up alongside I-17 near Cordes Junction (see Tour 6). On display are Soleri's designs for other futuristic skyscraper cities along with his famous windbells. Sales of the bells help finance Arcosanti. (No admission fee, but donations are accepted.)

On the southeast corner of Scottsdale and Indian Bend roads you encounter a unique park. It's called McCormick Railroad Park. It has a five-twelfths scale steam railroad (cars about 15 feet long and three and a half feet wide, modeled after actual trains) and an even smaller-scale railroad, both available for rides. There's a static display that includes a full-size old steam engine and a Pullman car (the latter was used by Presidents of the United States). There are other small model displays and two railroad stations. The land and rolling stock were donated by private individuals with a passion for railroads. You pay for rides, but the charge is small. Closed Mondays.

Go east on Indian Bend Road a half-mile or so to Hayden Road, turn south, and you're at the entry point to the Scottsdale Greenbelt. It's an exciting mix of fun and function. Back in the 1960s the United States Army Corps of Engineers proposed building a concrete-lined channel through Scottsdale to discharge the bedeviling floodwaters of Indian Bend Wash into the Salt River channel. Citizens of Scottsdale thought such a ditch would be as ugly as the Berlin Wall...literally and figuratively dividing the community. Out of their discussions with the Corps of Engineers came the greenbelt idea, and the result is lovely to behold: a seven-and-a-half-mile north-south strip of floodplain transformed into parks (no less than five), golf courses, bike paths, hiking trails, lakes for boating and fishing, tennis courts, swimming pools, picnic areas, and athletic arenas.

Go west to the center of Scottsdale via Indian School Road and south on Civic Center Plaza (two streets before Scottsdale Road) to take in a variety of sights: the Scottsdale Mall (a terraced park in the heart of downtown), the Scottsdale Center for the Arts, and a gleaming white City Hall complex designed by one of the valley's better-known architects, Bennie Gonzales. There's also a sculpture garden at Civic Center with works by well-known sculptors such as Louise Nevelson, John Waddell, and Dale Wright.

Just west of the mall is Old Scottsdale with — in addition to an array of stores — an 1880 blacksmith shop, a mission church, and an old red schoolhouse. The latter two have been restored and are headquarters respectively for the Scottsdale Symphony and Scottsdale Chamber of Commerce.

Scottsdale is also the hub of the Valley's resort industry (fine hotels on both sides of Scottsdale Road and extending westward into Paradise Valley). Shops are clustered in such enclaves as Marshall Way, Fifth Avenue, Main Street West, Camelview Plaza, Stetson Drive, Fashion Square, Old Scottsdale, and the Borgata. Red trolleys (trolley car bodies on truck chassis) shuttle tourists among the hotels and shopping centers.

Founded in 1891 by Winfield Scott, Scottsdale has grown from a small farming and ranching town to become a chic destination for many visitors to Arizona. Scottsdale offers a host of fine resorts, hotels, restaurants, boutiques, galleries and numerous Southwestern-flavored events such as the Parada del Sol (Parade of the Sun). Dick Dietrich/J. Peter Mortimer photos

Leaving Scottsdale, head south on Scottsdale Road, turn west on McDowell Road, then south again at 64th Street (which is also Galvin Parkway) to the entrance to the Desert Botanical Garden. It's as complete and diverse a collection of cacti, succulents, and desert flowers as is to be seen anywhere. There's much more than the familiar saguaro, barrel cactus, and cholla of the Arizona desert. In fact, Arizona cacti make up only 10 percent of the collection. Did you ever see, for instance, a totem pole cactus, native to Baja California, with a surface like melted wax and protrusions resembling Roman noses? Or a boojum tree, likewise from Baja, resembling an upside-down parsnip? It grows as tall as 70 feet in the wild.

More than 1000 different plants from the arid lands of the world are in the botanical garden, which draws more than 100,000 visitors a year. Ask for a self-guided tour booklet. There's a charge for that and admission into the garden.

Back to Galvin Parkway and a short distance south to the Phoenix Zoo. Many residents of the Valley don't realize that these 125 acres of mammals, reptiles, birds, and whatnot constitute the largest privately-owned, self-supporting zoo in the United States. No tax money, in other words. And the zoo, though not as large and rich as San Diego's, has made its own mark in world zoodom. It did so by taking a key part in the successful global effort to save the Arabian oryx. The oryx is a graceful gazelle-like creature with two straight parallel horns which, seen in profile, look like a single horn and may have given rise to the myth of the unicorn. It was hunted almost to

extinction in Africa. Because of Arizona's similar climate, a few surviving animals were shipped to the Phoenix Zoo. Breeding began, the progeny were sent back out to zoos throughout the world, and the oryx's survival seems assured. The zoo charges admission, of course.

Depart the zoo south to Van Buren Street, turn left for a short distance and turn right at Project Drive, to the Hall of Flame. It's the largest and most complete fire museum in the world, the brainchild of a devoted fire buff and businessman named George F. Getz, Jr. It started when he remarked lightly to his wife that it would be nice to have a fire engine for their kids to ride around in. On Christmas morning in 1951 he found a 1924 fire engine parked in his driveway. His collection grew, and now at the Hall of Flame (official sponsor: National Historical Fire Foundation) you'll find such firefighting oddities as: an English 1725 hand pumper, an 1870 hose carriage, a 1910 horse-drawn chemical wagon, and a hand pumper built by a friend of Paul Revere. There are more than 100 pieces of equipment in all. Admission charge. Closed on Sundays.

A side trip to Arizona State University in nearby Tempe might be in order here. It's the state's largest; indeed, its enrollment is one of the largest in the United States. The vast majority of its students commute from all parts of the Valley.

Go back to Van Buren Street and head eastward across the Salt River bridge into Tempe. That puts you on Mill Avenue. Stay on Mill Avenue until you reach the campus. (You can pick up a visitors guide at the information desk in the Memorial Union at the center of the campus. They

will have a schedule of events and a map.)

The Gammage Center for the Performing Arts, where Mill Avenue turns into Apache Boulevard, is well worth a visit. With its desert coloring, graceful globe-lighted ramps and contour curtains integrated into the exterior design, it is far and away the most outstanding of several Frank Lloyd Wright buildings scattered around the Phoenix area. Tours Tuesday, Thursday, and Saturday between 1:30 and 3:30 p.m. except when there are special events.

Leaving ASU to return to Phoenix, go back up Mill Avenue to the bridge, then west on Washington Street to Sixth Street and north a couple of blocks to the place where Phoenix recently began to discover that it had a past. The place is Heritage Square, at Sixth Street and Monroe. The city block of residential structures from the original townsite dates to the late 1800s. They might have been razed to make way for a parking lot had it not been for a former mayor named John Driggs, in company with a few other prescient civic leaders. They got the restoration going, and Heritage Square now contains a half-dozen interesting old homes and a Lathhouse Pavilion for meetings and celebrations. The best known of the dwellings is the mid-Victorian Rosson House, originally owned by a physician who was Phoenix mayor in 1895. The house looks for all the world like it was transplanted from San Francisco.

Just west of Heritage Square is the Phoenix Civic Plaza, with its lovely Symphony Hall and its John Waddell ballet sculptures. Twenty blocks farther west, off Washington Street, is the state capitol.

The capitol is not as prepossessing as some other state capitols, but there's a lot of history in it. An anchor from the battleship *U.S.S. Arizona*, sunk at Pearl Harbor at the beginning of World War II, is mounted at the east end of Capitol Mall, along with bronze plaques bearing the names of the sailors and marines who died in the attack. And in a small museum area is preserved an American flag with 45 stars that Teddy Roosevelt's Rough Riders carried up San Juan Hill in the Spanish-American War. Also: memorabilia of the Powell expedition that explored the Grand Canyon. An exhibit of vintage newspapers. The document proclaiming Arizona the 48th state, with the pen used by President Taft in signing it. And, by the way, there are 30,000 pounds of copper in the capitol dome (Arizona is, of course, the largest producer of copper among the states).

Your appropriate windup for a Valley of the Sun tour might be to get a sort of panoramic view of the Valley from South Mountain Park. It is easy to reach. From the heart of downtown Phoenix go south on Central Avenue about seven miles, and you'll drive right into the park.

It's the largest municipal park in the world (16,000 acres of carefully-preserved desert). There are prehistoric petroglyphs in the park, but what's really worth the trip is the view of the Phoenix area to be had from Dobbins Lookout, some 1200 feet above the city. Pick up a brochure at the gate (no admission charge) and follow the directions. You'll see planes landing at Sky Harbor International Airport, and from this vantage point the planes will be lower than you are. Catch the view of Phoenix toward dusk when the lights are coming on, and it'll be a sight worth writing home about.

This tour touches on only a few points of interest throughout the Valley. We suggest you contact the Phoenix and Valley of the Sun Convention and Visitors Bureau for a current schedule of events and a booklet. You'll find it varied and compelling.

(Above, left) The Rosson House, elegant "first lady of Heritage Square" in downtown Phoenix. The park was set aside as an authentic historical representation of turn-of-the-century Phoenix. Jerry Jacka photo

(Left) Nestled into the desert in east Phoenix, the Desert Botanical Garden cultivates an enormous variety of desert plants, both native and introduced, and is open to the public for daily tours and special exhibits. Lou Pardo photo

(Right) Winged Victory stands proudly (the statue is also a wind vane) atop the solid copper dome of the Arizona State Capitol in Phoenix. Built in 1900, the Capitol also houses a museum featuring early Arizona artifacts and documents. Nyle Leatham photo

FORT APACHE · CORONADO TRAIL · MOUNT GRAHAM

White Mountains · Eastern Arizona

The highlands....

What a magical thought! It conjures up mountains white in the winter, green in the summer. During those months when the desert simmers, the uplands beckon the camper, the backpacker, and the fisherman. And then from late fall to early spring the high country sends out irresistible invitations to the skier. Here, truly, the paradox of Arizona: wake up early during winter months, on a desert day that promises temperatures in the 70s, and a few hours later catch a chair lift to the top of a ski run.

For this tour we will use Globe as our point of departure, going out one way and coming back another. (If you're taking off from Phoenix or Tucson, allow a couple of extra hours for getting to Globe—via U.S. Route 60 from Phoenix; U.S. Route 89 and State Route 77 from Tucson.)

Head northeast out of Globe on a continuation of U.S. Route 60. Be prepared, some 35 miles out, for one of the state's major scenic surprises—the Salt River Canyon. It's on the state map. Written about and pictured in magazines and travel guides, it is—or seems to be—one of the big untold stories of Arizona travel. And so, almost without fail, travelers emit an involuntary gasp of astonishment as they round a curve and get their first glimpse of the gorge.

It bears a striking resemblance to the Grand Canyon—vertical rock walls, multicolored spires and buttes, lofty mesas, and, at the bottom, the Salt River winding southwestward toward Phoenix. It doesn't have the immensity of the Grand Canyon. But what it does have, and what the Grand Canyon lacks, is accessibility. You drive right down into it, dropping more than 2000 feet in five miles of swooping switchbacks. Then you cross a bridge and climb five miles out. There are plenty of turnout places for stopping and looking. Concrete steps have been installed near the bridge for walking down to the river bank, to a picnic area. And if you want to take the time, you can leave the highway just north of the bridge and drive a half-mile upstream on a dirt road to a waterfall.

(Left) The West Fork of the Little Colorado River meanders through the verdant highlands of the White Mountains. For many Arizonans the White Mountains provide a cool summertime retreat and wintertime playground featuring the state's largest skiing facility. Peter Kresan photo

(Above) General George Crook's quarters at Fort Apache. Built in 1883, today it is a museum for the Apache Culture Center. Fort Apache was the eastern terminus of Crook's Trail, a 175-mile road the General built across some of Arizona's toughest terrain during the Apache wars of the 1880s. Jerry Jacka photo

As you cross the Salt River bridge, you enter the Fort Apache Indian Reservation, often described as the largest privately-owned recreational area in the United States. It's the home of the White Mountain Apaches, who, when the reservation system came into being in the 19th century, found themselves occupying 1,664,872 acres of splendid wilderness—mountains, streams, lakes, timber, and grazing lands, plus the very real potential of oil, uranium, and other resources.

What's more, the Apaches know what to do with all this. They're timbering on a large scale. They're in the cattle business. And, under the aegis of the White Mountain Apache Recreation Enterprise, they've transformed their huge piece of real estate into a vacationers' paradise. Some half-million people a year take their pleasure—summer and winter—in that portion of the White Mountains that belongs to the Apaches. They fish 300-plus miles of trout streams and 26 lakes. They pitch tents or park their RVs on hundreds of campsites. They cut loose on the two-dozen or so ski runs of the Apache Sunrise Ski Resort. They hunt everything from quail to trophy elk. And all of this just within the confines of the Fort Apache Reservation. Note that a substantial portion of the White Mountains lies outside the reservation.

You can get into the White Mountains by either of two routes. Stay on U.S. Route 60 for another 50 miles past the Salt River Canyon until you reach a town with one of the quaintest names in the state. That's Show Low. (Genesis of that name: two early settlers were dissolving their ranching partnership by means of a winner-take-all game of cards. "Show low and you win," said one. The other showed a deuce of clubs and won the ranch, and Show Low the town became.)

From Show Low, you head southeastward on State Route 260 and start into the higher reaches of the White Mountains through the tandem summer resort communities of Lakeside and Pinetop. The countryside hereabouts is dotted with lakes bearing bucolic names like Rainbow and Woodland, and in recent years summer homes—mostly of southern Arizona folk—have sprouted in the Lakeside-Pinetop area like wild flowers after a wet winter.

The alternate route into the White Mountains is to leave U.S. Route 60, at a settlement called Carrizo, and execute a wide half-circle via State Route 73 through Fort Apache and Whiteriver.

Fort Apache dates to the Indian wars. It was established as a military base for the troops and scouts of General George Crook as they did battle with the intractable Indians. Today, drive through the preserved fortress and you'll feel that you've passed through a time warp into the last century. The buildings are—or seem—just as they were a hundred years ago. You'll see the quarters occupied by Crook. There's a museum. There's also an Indian boarding school currently in use.

Whiteriver, up the road four miles, is the tribal capital. Stop for a few minutes at the trading post. Then, beyond Whiteriver, turn east at Hon Dah (that's Apache for "Welcome") onto State Route 260. McNary, two miles farther, began in 1917 on property leased from the Apaches by Southwest Forest Industries. It was a typical company

(Right) Gahn (Apache Crown Dancers) appear at puberty rites and healing ceremonies as well as other events and celebrations. They represent "supernatural beings who live in the mountain caves and below the horizon in the cardinal directions."
Jerry Jacka photo

(Right, below) Autumn in the White Mountains from Green's Peak.
Wayne Davis photo

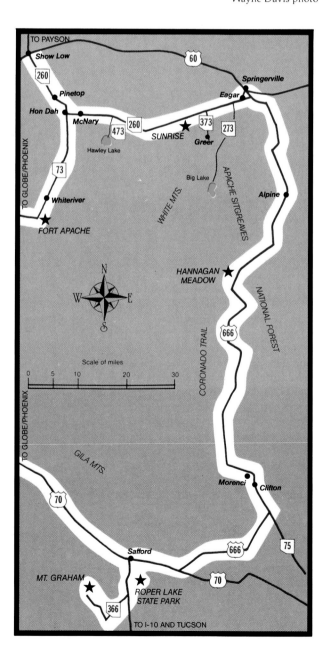

town until 1979 when fire took out the sawmill. Subsequently, Southwest rebuilt its lumber operations in Eagar, some 40 miles to the east. Today only a handful of people live on in the old company town that once had a population of 2000.

East of McNary, some eight miles, State Route 473 takes off towards one of the large, lovely reservoirs in this high country—Hawley Lake. Like so many others, it's a body of water impounded by one of a number of dams built by the Apaches. It's also one of the higher lakes in the state, at an elevation of about 8500 feet. The fishing is fine and, oh, it's cool in summer.

Go back to State Route 260 and another 10 miles east to the turnoff on State Route 273 to Sunrise, the Apache ski resort. It's a startling sight there in the high Whites—a brightly-painted, two-story lodge perched on a slope overlooking Sunrise Lake. The lodge has 100 rooms, dining and convention facilities, and an indoor swimming pool. About three miles away is the ski area (a shuttle bus goes every half-hour from the hotel during ski season, mid-November through Easter Sunday). At this writing the Apaches were operating 41 runs on three mountains (Sunrise and Apache peaks and Cyclone Circle), with 10 lifts—seven with chairs, three surface. Some of the runs have Apache names—Dishchii-bikoh (Red Valley), Na'ilihn (young girl), Goyaale (Geronimo). And the skiers come in droves, mainly from the Phoenix and Tucson areas.

The resort is designed not only to make money for the tribe but likewise to provide employment for its people.

Apaches work there in jobs at all levels, from manager to laborer.

Sunrise operates year-round (except for a cleanup period between Easter and May 20). Summer fun includes fishing, horseback riding, volleyball, canoeing, sailing, and sailboarding.

There are two other turnoffs from State Route 260 to interesting places, if you have the time: State Route 373 to Greer (fishing, camping, some lodging) and, seven miles farther, another segment of State Route 273 to Big Lake (more fishing and camping).

Note: if you're going fishing on the reservation, you'll need—in addition to an Arizona fishing license—a fishing permit from the White Mountain Apache Tribe and, if you're going after trout, an Arizona trout stamp. Same for hunting: state license and tribal permit. Licenses and permits are available at trading posts and stores throughout the White Mountains. And, as on any reservation, you need to bear in mind that you're subject to tribal law. Photographing Indians? Ask permission first. Pay if you're asked to do so.

State Route 260 ends just east of Eagar where it intersects U.S. Route 666 from Springerville, Eagar's sister town. Eagar was settled by Mormon pioneers and Springerville, it is said, by outlaws.

U.S. Route 666, the Coronado Trail, is one of Arizona's more scenic highways. It gets its name from the Spanish explorer Francisco Vásquez de Coronado. He was looking for the legendary Seven Cities of Cíbola, their streets and walls supposedly adorned with gold and jewels.

Mount Graham, in the Pinaleno Mountains, rises over 10,000 feet to form a forested island of green above the surrounding desert.
Ed Cooper photo

Actually they turned out to be Zuni villages, quite undecorated.

What you'll see along the Coronado Trail is Nature's own jewelry—immense forests of evergreen and aspen, great sweeps of meadowland, and mountain streams twinkling down the slopes toward the desert below. Twenty-five miles after you join U.S. Route 666 you'll reach Alpine, one of the high and handsome communities in Arizona at 8030 feet. This lush meadow was first settled by Anderson Bush and Elias Gibbs in 1877.

At Hannagan Meadow, south of Alpine, look closely: you just might see deer, elk, and wild turkey feeding. U.S. Route 666 carves a twisting path southward through the heart of the Apache Sitgreaves National Forest and over the Mogollon Rim. Be sure to stop at a turnout and take in the magnificent pine-and-aspen panorama below.

It's 123 miles from Eagar/Springerville to Clifton/Morenci. Allow yourself a good four hours or more, though. It's slow mountain driving much of the way. And in winter check road conditions. Sometimes the Coronado Trail closes because of snow.

Morenci is one of Arizona's major copper towns. Its open pit is the second largest in the United States (largest: Kennecott's Bingham Canyon in Utah) and third largest in the world. It is so enormous that, as you peer down from the observation point built for visitors by Phelps Dodge Corporation, the electric train and trucks on the terraced slopes below seem to be toys.

Southward some five miles from the mine is Morenci's copper-mining forerunner, Clifton, nestled in a mountain canyon. (Clifton was originally Cliff-town.) It traces its lineage to 1867 when Mexican miners panned gold from Chase Creek. The gold played out, but Clifton stays on.

Continue on U.S. Route 666 until it ties in with U.S. Route 70 to take you to Safford and then on back to Globe.

If you're allowing two days for this tour, you could have time for one more mountain expedition—into the upper reaches of 10,713-foot Mount Graham, near Safford. Though nearly a thousand feet shy of being as high as the highest of the White Mountains, Mount Baldy (11,403), Graham is more spectacular in two respects: (1) it stands alone, surging up from the desert floor like a mountainous sky island; (2) it is the loftiest place in Arizona where you can handily drive your car. The road nears 10,000 feet. Enjoy the convenience of a recreation area, campgrounds, and an 11-acre lake at Riggs Flat.

It is, inevitably, a summer refuge for folks living in and around Safford, Tucson, and other southeastern Arizona communities. And in the fall a hunter-in-a-hurry can drive into Graham, get his deer, and be back for lunch.

You can see what Mount Graham is all about by driving south out of Safford on U.S. Route 666 for nine miles and turning right onto State Route 366. It's called the Swift Trail (after a United States Forest Service supervisor of that name). It's paved to the top followed by several miles of good gravel road to the lake.

Indian Heritage

A thousand years ago there lived a race of people anthropologists today call the *Hohokam*. The word, from the language of the Pima Indians, means — depending on whom you ask to translate it — something on the order of "all used up." As the translation conveys, the Hohokam were a prehistoric people who came and went, and nobody knows exactly what happened to them or why they disappeared.

With this tour, then, we revisit those ancient people. This might be called an anthropological tour, but the word is so forbidding and the tour so engrossing and informative, let's just say that you're going to travel back down the trail of centuries. And while you're about it, you'll see not only the handiwork of the Hohokam but some of their 20th century successors as well.

To get an informational foundation for our tour, pause first in Phoenix, at the Heard Museum, 22 East Monte Vista Road, just off Central Avenue, not far from downtown. The Heard is one of the outstanding institutions of its kind in the nation. Named for its founders, Phoenix pioneers Dwight and Maie Bartlett Heard, it re-creates the Hohokam culture and way of life. At the same time it holds up a mirror to all of Southwestern Indian life. There are exhibits of Navajo weaving, Papago basketry, Zuñi jewelry...the list is almost endless. One of the major attractions is the Barry Goldwater collection of Kachina dolls, colorful religious symbols of the Hopi Indians. Another is the Fred Harvey collection of Indian arts and crafts. (Harvey was the pioneer who teamed up with the

Thought to be an ancient astronomical observatory built by the Hohokam culture, Casa Grande (Big House) Ruins National Monument rises above the desert floor. Evidence suggests the Hohokam were sophisticated astronomers able to predict spring and fall equinoxes and lunar eclipses. David Muench photo

Santa Fe Railroad to give early-day travelers access to the Grand Canyon's South Rim.) The Heard also has a gallery of contemporary Indian art from the brushes of such celebrated painters as Fritz Scholder, R. C. Gorman, and Oscar Howe. There's an admission fee.

In a newly-built section doubling the size of the Heard you can see an exciting nine-projector multimedia show, "Voices of Our Land." And Heard has an annual Indian fair in March.

Go south on Central Avenue, to Jefferson Street. Turn left. It's a one-way street going east, and just past 24th Street it merges with Washington Street, which will take you to Pueblo Grande Museum at 4619 East Washington. This is not only an exhibit devoted to the Hohokam—it's where the Hohokam actually lived, settling here near the bank of the Salt River some 10 centuries ago. Pueblo Grande included homes, storerooms, a ball court, and a platform mound. The City of Phoenix maintains the museum and has supervised the excavations for years.

But the Hohokam left behind more than a ball court and a platform mound. They developed a network of hundreds of miles of canals—the largest prehistoric irrigation system in North America. It was so well laid out that

(Right and below) Regarded as the finest museum of its type, the Heard Museum in central Phoenix features traditional Southwestern Native American arts and crafts—from prehistoric to contemporary. Items such as Dineh by Allan Houser (right) and the Ahola-chief Kachina from the Barry Goldwater Collection are representative of the Heard's fine quality collections.
Jerry Jacka photos

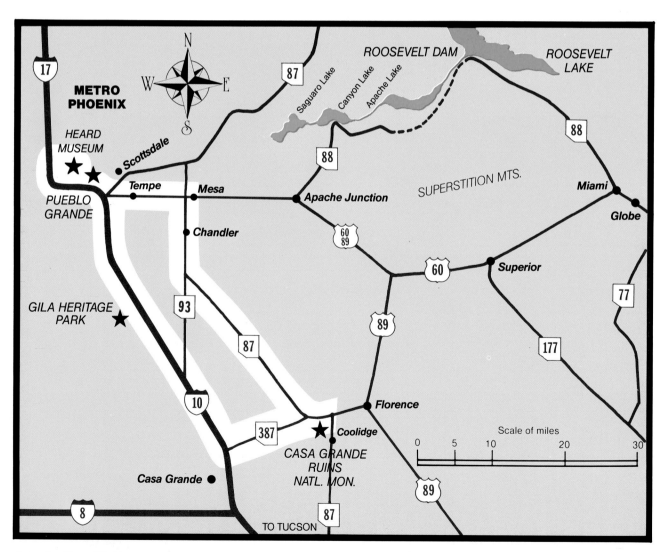

engineers centuries later used it as a basis for planning the complex irrigation system which waters modern Phoenix and surroundings.

The Hohokam disappeared around A.D. 1450, and their fate has provoked much scholarly conjecture. Likely they weren't driven away by enemies. Rather it is felt their irrigation system was damaged by fierce summer thunderstorms; soil in the fields played out, followed by 30 years of drought. But these are questions the anthropologists are still studying.

There's a fee for admission to Pueblo Grande.

Go back to 44th Street and turn south on the Hohokam Expressway, which takes you to Interstate 10 (take the East on-ramp) for another milestone on our trail back through the centuries. That is the Gila Heritage Park, on the Gila River Indian Reservation, 25 miles to the southeast (Exit 175, Casa Blanca off-ramp). Heritage Park and the adjoining Gila River Arts and Crafts Center are projects aimed at making tribal members more self-sufficient.

Here you see a re-creation of the earthen-and-reed pit houses typical of Hohokam dwellings occupied about the time Charlemagne fought the Saxons. There are also artifacts of more contemporary tribes—Pima, Papago, Maricopa, and Apache—showing the imaginative ways they adapted to desert life. Storyboards explain.

The crafts center, a modern white building standing agleam against the desert background, features the handicrafts of numerous Southwestern tribes. Indian artists and crafts men and women demonstrate their work. And there's a coffee shop where you can buy fry bread — deep-fried raised flour dough cake — and other ethnic delicacies.

There's an admission charge at Gila Heritage Park.

Return to the interstate and proceed south another 20 miles to the exit that takes you onto State Route 387. It's 15 miles from there to Coolidge and Casa Grande Ruins National Monument.

This is the celebrated four-story house of the Hohokam, discovered in 1694 by Father Kino, who built Mission San Xavier del Bac near Tucson (see Tour 13). Casa Grande was erected around A.D. 1350 and is quite unlike other Hohokam buildings, bearing a greater resemblance, in fact, to pueblo-like structures found in northern Arizona and New Mexico. The big mystery about the Big House (the translation of Casa Grande from Spanish) is simply: what was it? multi-storied dwelling? lookout tower? fortress or watchtower for defense against adversaries?

One rather new and intriguing theory is that it may have been used for astronomical observations. Several round holes in the walls of the upper chambers seem to relate to movements of the sun and stars. Might the Hohokam have used astronomical sightings to schedule their planting seasons or ceremonial events?

Today, Casa Grande's adobe mud walls are sheltered under a big metal cover. There's a visitors center, and you can follow a self-guiding trail through the ruins. Admission fee is charged.

Return to Phoenix by a different route, State Route 87 northward through Chandler, one of the fast-growing satellite cities near Phoenix.

(Above) A Pueblo Indian dancer at O'odham Tash (Pima/Papago Days in the Papago language), the annual three-day festival in Casa Grande. Each February more than 90,000 Indians and non-Indians from all over the United States gather here for parades, barbecues, crafts displays, dances, and the largest all-Indian rodeo in the nation. James Tallon photo

(Above, right) Displaying arts and crafts from nearly every Southwestern Indian tribe, the Gila River Arts and Crafts Center, owned by the Pima Tribe, also features Gila Heritage Park with full-size replicas of Pima, Papago, Maricopa, Apache, and Hohokam villages; a restaurant specializing in American, Mexican, and Indian foods; and an indoor museum of the Pima and Maricopa Indian tribes. Jerry Jacka photo

(Right) Water jars, bowls of corn and wild beans, and a mortar and pestle, all from the Casa Grande Ruins National Monument collection, were common items to Arizona's desert tribes during prehistoric times. Jerry Jacka photo

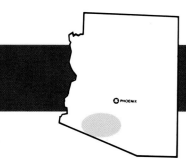

Papagoland

This is the Sonoran Desert, and it's quintessential desert—as vast, rugged, and arid an expanse as you're likely to encounter in the New World. It stretches across the southwesternmost half of the state and southward into Sonora, Mexico.

Starting from Tucson, take Interstate 19 to the Ajo Way turnoff. That puts you on State Route 86 heading west, and 56 miles farther you're at the Kitt Peak Road. Atop this rocky "sky island" sits one of the remarkable astronomical observatories in the world. It's open to the public without charge every day except Christmas Eve and Christmas Day, and a half-million visitors annually drive up the winding scenic road to the observatory summit.

Kitt Peak is in the Quinlan Mountains, rising nearly 4000 feet above the desert floor, in the heart of the 3-million-acre Papago Indian Reservation. A dozen miles south is Baboquivari Peak, which is sacred to the Papagos. Understandably, they were leery of letting "the men with long eyes" mount their complicated telescopes so close. In the final arrangement for use of Kitt Peak, astronomers pledged that all caves on Kitt Peak would be off limits. The Papagos felt their deity, I'itoi (ee-ee-toy), who lives on Baboquivari and is believed sometimes to take the form of a coyote, might want to visit Kitt Peak and need a den in which to hide or get in out of the weather.

The Papago Reservation, east of Quijotoa. They call themselves O'odham but outside of their southern Arizona reservation, second largest in the United States, they are the Papago. An ancient and successful desert people, they have adapted to modern ways but retain their own unique view of the world. Jerry Jacka photo

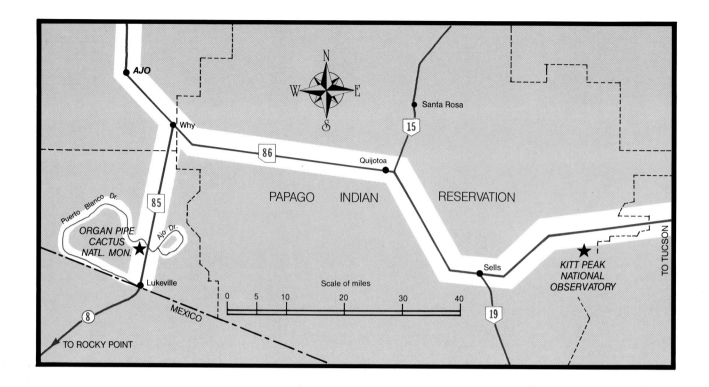

Kitt Peak is a national observatory, the site having been chosen because of the clarity of the air and the distance from intrusive city light. It's one of the National Optical Astronomy Observatories (NOAO) operated by the Association of Universities for Research in Astronomy (AURA). More than a dozen universities are involved in AURA, which maintains the observatories under contract to the National Science Foundation. Sixty percent of Kitt Peak's telescope time is given over to visiting astronomers from all over the world.

Perched there on top of the mountain is the world's largest collection of telescopes—18 in all. One is the McMath solar telescope, biggest of its kind anywhere—a triangular-shaped structure that looks rather like a figure 7 lying on its side. It was built especially for studies of the sun and is so designed as to beam light down a 500-foot shaft to mirrors. Three-fifths of the shaft is underground. The solar telescope was named for Dr. Robert R. McMath of the University of Michigan, first president of AURA.

And then there's the huge dome-shaped Mayall four-meter telescope, 19 stories high, fourth largest of its type in the world. (Dr. Nicholas U. Mayall was director of the observatory from 1960 until 1971.) The Mayall's 156-inch mirror is so powerful that, given the right conditions, astronomers could read a newspaper in the New York Times building. The $10 million telescope and its mounting weigh 375 tons, but are so delicately balanced that accurate tracking of the stars is made possible with a small one-half horsepower motor. Using the Mayall, astronomers study objects billions of light years away and more than 6 million times fainter than the dimmest star visible to the naked eye.

At the observatory you'll find a visitors gallery with special non-glare glass to enhance picture-taking. No food is sold, but there's a picnic area with tables, benches, and fire pits.

Kitt Peak hours are 10 a.m. to 4 p.m.

A word of caution: a visit to Kitt Peak on a wet winter day can be dangerous. What you see as rain on the desert becomes snow as you climb the mountain, and suddenly you're driving up an icy road. If in doubt, call ahead: (602) 623-5796, extension 250.

And now back down the mountain and on to the west. You'll go through Sells, the Papago agency town. If you want to stop and shop, the Papago specialty is hand-woven basketry along with mats, trays, and the like. There's a trading post in Sells, and another one 22 miles westward, at Quijotoa.

Thirty-seven miles beyond Quijotoa, State Route 86 joins State Route 85 at a little settlement with the curious name of Why. Why Why? The name derived from the days when motorists called it "The Y." Turn south on State Route 85. Within a half-dozen miles you'll reach the northern boundary of Organ Pipe Cactus National Monument, and 15 miles farther down the road is the visitors center. Unlike other national monuments, there is no admission charge at this one, the state's largest.

Adjoining the border with Mexico, Organ Pipe is 516 square miles of pristine desert. It's nearly half the size of the state of Rhode Island, and larger than Rocky Mountain National Park in Colorado or the Great Smoky Mountains National Park of North Carolina and Tennessee. Organ Pipe gets its name from the curious species of cactus that grows in profusion throughout the area. The cactus resembles the saguaro, but where the saguaro usually has a single main trunk with arms jutting out, the

organ pipe forms a cluster of trunks resembling huge organ pipes as high as 18 or 20 feet. It is found only here and in adjoining Mexico.

Another interesting species found within the monument, a close relative of the organ pipe, is the senita cactus. It looks like the organ pipe, but its stem has fewer ribs, and near the tip of each stem are whiskery spines resembling an old man's beard. Hence the name *senita*, Spanish for "old one." There are, in all, 29 different types of cacti in this remote desert wonderland, plus some 250 species of birds and a great variety of desert animals.

The monument area gets scant rainfall, except in abnormal years. And, historically, this was the route of *El Camino del Diablo* (The Devil's Highway) of early-day travelers. Padre Kino pioneered a path across this formidable stretch of Sonoran Desert when he traveled from Sonoita, Mexico, to the present-day site of Yuma, Arizona. Between 1849 and 1860, California's gold-seekers traveled The Devil's Highway. Authorities estimate some 300 perished here.

Tarry a few minutes at the visitors center to pick up brochure guides and see the slide shows that tell the story of Organ Pipe Cactus National Monument. Don't be disappointed if you see only one or two organ pipes in the immediate vicinity. Travel the scenic loop drives—one or another or, conceivably, both—and you'll see organ pipes aplenty.

Both loop drives begin at the visitors center. One is the Ajo Mountain Drive, a 21-mile one-way road (gravel, but graded and well-maintained) east—into the Ajo range and back to the visitors center. The other is longer—a 51-mile route westward, known as the Puerto Blanco Drive, circling the Puerto Blanco Mountains and skirting

Kitt Peak National Observatory, from the catwalk of the McMath solar telescope. Atop the mountain stands the world's largest collection of telescopes — a total of 18. They are used by astronomers from many countries.

Gary Ladd photo

the Mexican border before rejoining State Route 85 at the southern end of the monument. It has historic significance, since part of it parallels the route of the early-day desert travelers. Then, too, it is only the Puerto Blanco Drive that affords you a glimpse of the rare senita cactus. It also brings you to Quitobaquito Springs, a kind of mini-oasis which is at the same time the jumping off point for El Camino del Diablo and a bird-watcher's paradise.

If you need to complete this tour in one day, the shorter of the two loops is recommended. You see lots of organ pipe and cholla cactus. Cholla look soft and furry but that "fur" is really a mass of tiny spikes that break off on

(Left) A Papago basket weaver expresses herself through original forms and designs. The basket "supermarket" on the reservation is the trading post. Four are currently active: Santa Rosa, Quijotoa, Sells, and Pisinimo. James Tallon photo

(Right) Organ Pipe Cactus National Monument and the curiously-shaped cactus which gave it its name. This 515-square-mile region is distinct from all other deserts because only here does the Mexican-Sonoran desert intrude into the United States. Spring is the season to see it at its best. Gary Ladd photo

(Below) Baboquivari Peak is at the center of the universe, say the Papago. It is also from this mountain, they believe, that the spirit of goodness watches over them. David Muench photo

slightest contact and embed in clothes, flesh, and dog fur. (The most useful first aid instruments for cactus injury are a comb and pliers.)

The road gives you an exciting view of massive canyon walls and even a natural stone arch 36 feet high and 90 feet wide.

There are campsites and an RV park about a mile and a half southwest of the visitors center. The monument headquarters has no lodging or dining facilities, but there are picnic benches, and you can find a small motel and store at Lukeville, five miles south.

(Above) Gambel's quail. A pleasant fellow to encounter while hiking, or slowly driving through Organ Pipe Cactus National Monument. But to really participate in a birding event, stop at Quitobaquito Springs where there is a perennial water supply and lots of other birds. The monument has over 250 recorded bird species.

Jerry Sieve photo

(Right) Owl clover in spring carpets the desert along Ajo Mountain Drive. Shortest of the monument's two scenic roads, the drive is coordinated with self-guiding tour booklets which familiarize visitors with a variety of desert plants. The 21-mile loop road travels close to the fantastically shaped Ajo Range.

Jerry Sieve photo

Incidental note: if you have a choice, visit Organ Pipe in March or April after a moist Arizona winter. The desert wild flowers will knock your eyes out.

Another incidental note: if you're camping out or traveling in an RV, you might consider staying overnight at Organ Pipe campground and heading out to Ajo early the next morning for what could be a charming train ride if circumstances permit. Ajo is 10 miles north of Why on State Route 85, and the train ride is on what rail buffs call the Ajo Cannonball, more properly known as the Tucson, Cornelia and Gila Bend Railroad. When Ajo's big copper producer, the New Cornelia Mine, is in operation, the Ajo Cannonball runs between Ajo and Gila Bend. (The mine was closed at this writing because of the state of the copper market, and the train was operating only intermittently.) One of the few remaining mixed trains in the West (freight and passengers), it leaves Ajo with loads of copper concentrate at 6:30 a.m. and connects with the Southern Pacific at Gila Bend. Then it returns with loads of other products for the mine. Passengers (limit: 18) ride in the caboose. The fare is extremely modest — best travel bargain west of Staten Island. Call or write ahead to see if the train is running: Agent, Tucson, Cornelia and Gila Bend Railroad, 1 Plaza, Ajo, AZ 85321. Telephone (602) 387-6068.

Tucson West

(Left) "Two hundred years ago there appeared at Bac a church of unearthly beauty. Framed in the warm browns of the surrounding hills and the violet shadows of distant mountains, it rises today brilliantly white from the desert floor.... That church, popularly known as 'the White Dove of the Desert,' is Mission San Xavier del Bac." Father Kieran McCarty, Arizona Highways, *January, 1978.* Dick Dietrich photo

(Above) Byzantine and Moorish elements are fused into a unified design in the interior of San Xavier, a building authorities claim is the finest example of mission architecture in the United States. Jerry Jacka photo

There are so many places of interest in Tucson that we've divided the area in two. This tour is to the west of the city.

We suggest you allow at least a full day, visiting Mission San Xavier del Bac and Old Tucson in the morning and devoting the afternoon, or most of it, to the Arizona-Sonora Desert Museum. (You could spend an entire day at the museum. Many do.)

The famous mission of San Xavier is situated on the San Xavier Indian Reservation, nine miles south of the city. Take Interstate 19 (the freeway to Nogales) southward to the mission turnoff, then head west. Well before you reach it you'll see the stunning white twin-towered edifice rising majestically from the brown/green floor of the desert. You can readily understand why it is called the "White Dove of the Desert."

San Xavier is universally acclaimed as the finest example of mission architecture in the United States. Its founder was the great Italian-born Jesuit explorer-priest Father Eusebio Francisco Kino. He spent 22 of his 66 years mapping the uncharted desert in this region he called *Pimería Alta,* "the Highlands of the Pima," instructing Indians in the skills of farming and ranching, and establishing a chain of missions.

The site of this mission was an Indian village called Bac that Kino first visited in 1692. The original mission, which Kino named to honor his chosen patron, St. Francis Xavier, was located two miles north of the present site. Apaches destroyed it, and Franciscans built the present mission in the late 18th century.

The architecture is a mix of Moorish, Byzantine, and late Mexican. Oddly, one of the two towers has not been completed. Two explanations are heard: (1) that the Spaniards laid a heavy tax on completed churches, and so the mission was never finished; (2) that the mission's architect was killed in a fall from one of the belfries and, in his memory, a belfry was left incomplete.

The area behind the altar, underneath the great dome of the church, was originally a dazzling gilt color, although it has faded with the passing years. A statue of St. Francis Xavier rises above the main altar. Two wooden lions

(Right) The Wild West still lives at Old Tucson, where countless movie and television cowboys have died with their boots on.
James Tallon photo

(Far right) Tucson, a community of over a half-million people, has seen considerable growth since it became a walled city in 1776. Today, the Old Pueblo continues to draw visitors and new residents that swell its borders. What are the attractions? Author C. L. Sonnichsen sums them up perfectly in Tucson — The Life and Times of an American City: *"It's a somewhat spiney and superheated corner of Paradise."*
Kathleen Norris Cook photo

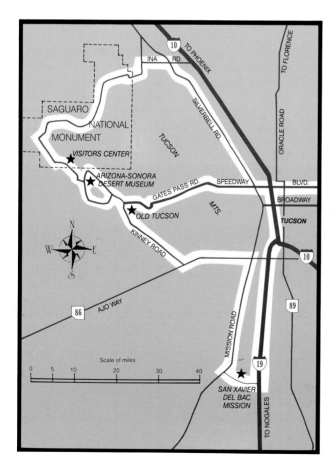

standing on the sides of the communion rail, representing the Lions of Castile, honor the reigning Spanish family of the late 18th century. Almost every square foot of interior surface is decorated with statuary or painting.

West of the mission is a mortuary chapel and beyond that an old cemetery, many of its graves unmarked.

The mission is open every day from 8 a.m. to 6 p.m.

A taped lecture comes over loudspeakers and is played about every 20 minutes (except during mass). A gift shop inside sells Papago crafts and religious articles. No fee is charged for admission to San Xavier, although donations are welcome.

If you're in the neighborhood on the first Friday after Easter, you might take in the annual San Xavier Fiesta. It features a pageant commemorating the founding of the mission, complete with mounted Spanish horsemen, robed priests, a hundred mesquite bonfires, Papago dancing, and craft and food booths.

As you leave the mission, pick up Mission Road north to Ajo Way (State Route 86) and turn westward for a few miles. Then, on the first paved road to the right, which is Kinney Road, take off into Tucson Mountain Park and the western segment — or Tucson Mountain Unit — of Saguaro National Monument.

Near the junction with Gates Pass Road, coming out from Tucson, you'll see Old Tucson on your right. Another make-believe Western town and movie set. Here you can watch a Western movie or television segment being shot.

The set was built by Columbia Pictures in 1939 as a replica of Tucson during the frontier era for a big-budget film called *Arizona*, starring William Holden and Jean Arthur.

Old movie sets aren't supposed to die. They just rot away. But this one did neither. An indefatigable Western

buff named Robert Shelton picked it up, refurbished it, and reopened it as a combination movie location and amusement park. John Wayne made *Rio Bravo* here. Frank Sinatra came around to shoot *Dirty Dingus McGee*. Clint Walker did *Death of a Gunfighter*. More than a hundred films and scores of TV shows and commercials have been filmed at Old Tucson—most of the time with tourists looking on, being appropriately shushed by nervous directors.

What you will find here, besides the false fronts of Dodge City, are a narrow gauge railroad and a stagecoach to ride on, the obligatory fake gunfights in front of the old saloon, and miscellaneous items from that era such as a butterchurn, foot-warmer, and high-top shoes. Nearby are antique stores and novelty shops.

There's an admission charge to Old Tucson.

Go back to Kinney Road and on through the saguaro forest a few miles to the Arizona-Sonora Desert Museum. Don't let that word museum fool you. It's far more than that—it's an innovative, exciting mix of museum, zoo, botanical garden, and aquarium. (Yes, there are things that swim in the desert country. Like otters, fish, and beaver.)

The museum has a mission: to tell the story of the Sonoran Desert—its flora, its animal life, and its geology—with the hope that people, knowing the wonders of the desert, will help preserve them.

And the museum (which, by the way, is privately funded) does such a good job that when the British Broadcasting Corporation set about to film the seven outstanding zoos of the world, two in the United States were picked. San Diego was one. The Arizona-Sonora Desert Museum was the other.

The museum keeps as few creatures in cages as necessary.

Mostly they live in re-created natural-looking habitats. The desert bighorn sheep, for instance, have their own private mountainside.

You'll see such desert marvels as birds that make their home in cacti, somehow avoiding impalement on the sharp thorns, and the kangaroo rat, which never takes a drink of water. (It extracts hydrogen and oxygen from carbohydrates in dry seeds and recombines them into what is called the "water of metabolism.")

The newest and most striking of all the museum's exhibits is the Congdon Earth Sciences Center, illustrating vividly the dynamic forces that shaped this desert region. One section of the center is an imitation of a limestone cave, complete with stalactites and stalagmites. You'll see realistic fossils embedded in the texture of the cave. And, stamina and dexterity permitting, you can go spelunking through a maze of side passages.

The other section of the Earth Sciences Center consists of two rooms of exhibits showing how the Sonoran Desert was formed, taking the viewer back billions of years in geologic time. There are films, photographs, maps, plant-animal-and-fossil displays, and, overhead, color transparencies of the heavens, some of them taken at nearby Kitt Peak National Observatory. In another room are minerals and gems of the desert. On a huge screen you see a volcano in full eruption. There's a beautiful desert garden, as well as a walk-in aviary, and a tortoise enclosure where you can touch the unflappable desert tortoise.

The museum charges an admission fee.

You can go back to Tucson via Gates Pass Road (it brings you out on West Speedway), or you can continue on through Saguaro National Monument on Kinney Road. Several excellent loop drives return you to Tucson via Ina Road and Interstate 10.

Suzanne Clemenz

James Tallon

Jeff Gnass

(Left) A desert plant par excellence is the saguaro. At maturity it may stand 50 feet high and weigh 10 tons. But it begins life small, usually in the shade of another plant. In 25 years it will stand two feet in height. Arms may not develop until the plant celebrates its golden anniversary. Then, somewhere between 100 and 150 years, old age arrives and the saguaro may have as many as 35 to 40 arms. Jeff Gnass photo

(Above) The Arizona-Sonora Desert Museum is rated among the top seven zoos in the world. Latest addition to the 12-acre facility is the Steven H. Congdon Earth Sciences Center, where visitors enter "real" limestone caves to see Nature at work deep below the earth.

Tucson East

What many Arizona visitors and residents don't realize, this relatively new state (the last of the contiguous states to be admitted to the Union) has a very old city. That city is Tucson, which is one of the older continuously inhabited cities in America. The Old Pueblo, as residents like to call it, has seen a succession of civilizations—Indians, Spaniards, Mexicans, pioneers, and now more than a half-million modern-day Americans.

It seems fitting, therefore, to start this city tour where Tucson itself started—in the downtown area. This is where the original walled Presidio of San Agustín del Tucson was built by Spaniards in 1776. Pick up a self-guided walking tour brochure at the Metropolitan Tucson Convention and Visitors Bureau in La Placita Village at 120 West Broadway. And while you're there, get a map of Tucson.

With a growing sense of its heritage, Tucson has designated several areas as historically significant to make sure that fine old adobe buildings are preserved. One worth visiting is the Edward Nye Fish house at North Main and Alameda. It is now part of the Tucson Museum of Art complex, which comprises the northern portion of the presidio. Fish established a merchandising business in Tucson in the 1860s and erected a fine home with two-and-one-half-foot-thick adobe walls and 15-foot ceilings. President and Mrs. Rutherford B. Hayes were entertained here. The Fishes' daughter, Clara, was the first student registered at the University of Arizona. Their home, and that of their next door friend, Hiram Sanford Stevens, formed the social center of 19th century Tucson.

Also part of the art museum complex is La Casa Córdova, one of the oldest surviving buildings in Tucson. It's in the National Register of Historic Places. You'll see old pottery and tools used by Mexican residents along with dried food stored in Pima Indian ceramic jars.

There's an attractive and memorable historic plaza in downtown Tucson, between the modern city hall and the Pima County courthouse with its multihued mosaic dome. Plaza de Las Armas was used by the Spaniards for military formations, drills, and fiestas.

The Arizona Historical Society Museum and Library might be your next stop. It's at 949 East Second Street

(Above) Tucson has been home to Spanish explorers, colonizing priests, and trappers. Today, Tucson's half-million inhabitants live in a more settled environment where resorts and dude ranches are major attractions.
Carlos Elmer photo

(Right) Yesterday and today, the old and the new—each complements the other in the heart of Tucson. At left in photo, Pima County Courthouse, with its rich tapestry of Spanish Colonial styling, glows in the warm desert sun beside the clean lines of steel and glass skyscrapers of this modern-day city.
Ray Manley photo

across from the west side of the University of Arizona. There are exhibits portraying Arizona's past, beginning with the Indians and the arrival of the Spaniards, and rooms that reproduce a home as it looked at the turn of the century, with parlor, library, bedroom, dining room, and kitchen. An exhibit of an old copper mine includes the shaft, miners' camp, and all. You'll also see antique cars, a stagecoach, a fire engine, and more. The society's library contains an extensive collection of early documents, newspapers, photographs, and the like. Admission to the museum and library is free.

Parking is difficult at the university, so you might leave your car near the Historical Society while you go afoot to browse around the campus. A block west of the university's Park Avenue boundary, at 843 East University, is the Center for Creative Photography. It includes the lifetime works of such noted photographers as Ansel Adams, W. Eugene Smith, Edward Weston, Wynn Bullock, Aaron Siskind, Harry Callahan, and Frederick Sommer. Admission to exhibits is free.

Just inside the main gate of the university, on either side of the street, are the two sections of the Arizona State Museum. You can see a magnificent collection of Southwestern archeology featuring displays of aboriginal cultures dating back a hundred centuries. There are also dioramas, sand paintings, and a gallery of primitive art. No charge for admission.

North of the museum some three blocks, at the corner of Speedway and Olive, is the university's Museum of Art. You might not expect to see art treasures such as Tintoretto, Rodin, and Degas in a university museum in Arizona, but here they are. And there's one of the finest of the several fine art collections of S.H. Kress, the five-and-dime magnate, housed here. Free admission.

You might retrieve your car now and drive to the east side of the campus (parking is sort of catch-as-catch-can anywhere around the university). At the corner of Cherry Avenue and the University Mall is the Grace Flandrau Planetarium, which symbolizes the fact that the university is a major world center for astronomical research. In the planetarium there's a 16-inch telescope available for free public viewing from dusk to 10 p.m., weather permitting. There are hour-long space and star shows in a 50-foot domed theater, plus displays of the sun and solar system, the Milky Way, meteorites, and astronomical art. At the south entrance to the planetarium you'll find a blue sundial known as an analemma. Your shadow indicates the time in hours and minutes.

The Flandrau Planetarium has been described aptly as "the perfect environment for communicating science to a

(Left) The main entrance of the Arizona Historical Society headquarters in Tucson. The portal and rose window are from Arizona's first Roman Catholic cathedral, San Agustín, completed in 1883.
Peter Kresan photo

(Above) The Grace Flandrau Planetarium at the University of Arizona offers a variety of dramatic public shows, educational programs, science hall exhibits, and other facilities (including a 16-inch telescope on the roof) to interested visitors of all ages.
Jack Dykinga photo

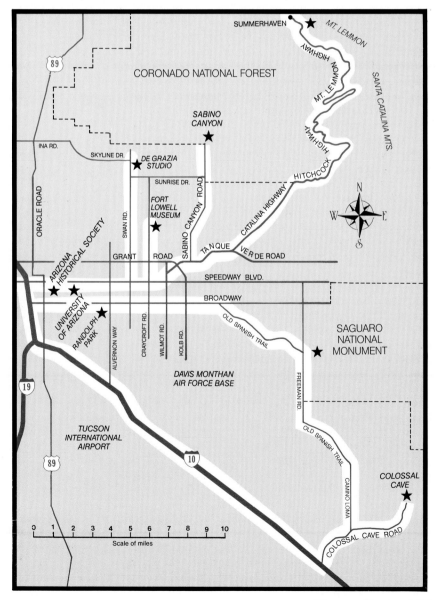

non-science-oriented public through the universal language of art."

Admission to the planetarium is free but there's a charge for the star show in the theater.

About a mile and a half southeast of the university is Randolph Park (parts of it are called Reid Park), a large expanse of greenery in a city with an otherwise pervasive flavor of the desert. It has a municipal golf course, a fine rose garden, a zoo, and a baseball field where the Cleveland Indians train in the spring.

Now consider the northeast part of Tucson. At 2900 North Craycroft Road (Craycroft and Fort Lowell Road) is the Fort Lowell Park and Museum. It's an old military base, active from 1873 to 1891, from which troops sallied forth to battle Geronimo and his Apache followers. The ruins of the original adobe hospital are there, along with the remains of several barracks buildings. The commanding officer's quarters have been reconstructed and now constitute the museum, furnished in the mode of 1886. The halls contain a display case of military uniforms and equipment, maps, photographs, and documents. There's no admission fee.

Farther north, in the foothills of the Santa Catalina Mountains, is Ted DeGrazia's Gallery in the Sun, at 6300 North Swan (Swan and Skyline Drive). In an adobe brick building are displayed the works of the late Southwestern artist whose paintings of angelic Hispanic and Indian children earned fame far beyond the borders of Arizona. Nearby, DeGrazia and his friends, the Yaqui Indians, built a mission in memory of Father Kino and dedicated it to the Virgin of Guadalupe. Admission to gallery and mission is free.

East of the DeGrazia gallery is the entrance to one of the places that Tucsonans love best—Sabino Canyon, in the Santa Catalina foothills. The canyon is a desert refuge of streams, waterfalls, hiking and biking trails, and picnic sites. You can drive to the visitors center, but then you have to walk from there or take the tram. There's a small charge for the tram.

Also in this northeastern section of Tucson begins the road to Mount Lemmon in the Santa Catalinas. (You'll need to allow the better part of a day for this side trip.) Instead of turning north on Sabino Canyon Road, continue east on Tanque Verde, as it winds into the Hitchcock Highway and starts up Mount Lemmon's south slope. It's a 30-mile trip—about an hour's drive—to the top of the 9157-foot mountain. Bear in mind that's very nearly 7000 feet above the desert floor, and it's this close juxtaposition of cool piney mountain range towering above warm cactus desert that gives Mount Lemmon a special appeal.

As you climb, you see the vegetation changing, from cactus and desert shrub through piñon and juniper to pine, fir and aspen. (You'd witness the same changes driving from southern Arizona to the Canadian border.) There are scenic pullouts, including one from which you can look north all the way to the copper smelter stacks of the San Pedro Valley.

In winter, when the snow is right, there's skiing on Mount Lemmon. It is, in fact, the southernmost ski area in the United States. The lift operates in summer for sightseeing.

(Right) Tucked away in Bear Canyon in the Santa Catalina Mountains north of Tucson, Seven Falls is the destination for one of the more popular hikes in the area. Hikers should leave cars at the Sabino Canyon parking area, climb aboard the U.S. Forest Service tram to lower Bear Canyon, and begin the 4.4 mile round trip trek from there. The hike guarantees beautiful scenery and wet feet—the trail crosses Bear Creek seven times before arriving at the falls.
David Muench photo

There are campgrounds and a small community called Summerhaven, with a lodge and cabins affording an escape from the desert summer below.

Two more places of interest are located in the eastern and southeastern parts of Tucson.

One is the eastern segment—properly called the Rincon Mountain Unit—of the Saguaro National Monument. (You can get there by going east on Broadway some eight or nine miles from downtown and picking up the Old Spanish Trail to the southeast.) There's a nine-mile drive that gives you a close look at desert growth against a scenic background of Mica Mountain and Rincon Peak. There's also a one-mile nature trail. (You can get a self-guiding leaflet at the visitors center.) No admission charge.

Colossal Cave is 22 miles southeast of downtown Tucson. Continue southeastward from Saguaro National Monument on Old Spanish Trail. It's the largest dry cave in the world, formed from limestone millions of years ago by the action of seeping water. Back in Arizona's lawless days it was a hideout for robbers. Nobody knows how far into the Rincon Mountains the cavern goes because it has not been fully explored. There's a constant underground temperature of 72 degrees. An admission fee is charged.

To get back to Tucson, continue southward to Interstate 10 and turn back west.

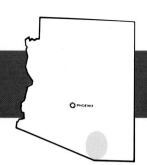

MADERA CANYON • TUBAC • TUMACACORI NATIONAL MONUMENT • MEXICO

Spanish Tradition

(Above) Jesuit missionary Father Eusebio Francisco Kino visited the site of Tumacacori in 1691 and established it as one of his 24 missions in northern Mexico. The present adobe structure was built by the Franciscans and took more than 20 years to erect. It was abandoned in 1848 as a result of the Apache Indians' reign of terror. The United States government declared it a national monument in 1908. James Tallon photo

(Left) Madera Canyon, famous for its variety of rare bird life, bursts into fall color. David Muench photo

This part of Arizona is heavily flavored with Spanish sauce. From beginning to end, the southward leg of this tour has a pervasive Spanish influence. Tucson...ancient Spanish presidio. Tubac...Spanish garrison of the 18th century. Tumacacori...link in the long chain of Padre Kino missions. The border twin cities of Nogales, Arizona, and Nogales, Mexico, where Spanish and English blend in a language we had to find a word for — Spanglish.

Even Green Valley, the first point of interest to catch your attention as you spin down Interstate 19 from Tucson, carries a Spanish patina. It was designed as a retirement community with tile-roofed colonial architecture against a backdrop of the Sonoran Desert and Santa Rita Mountains.

At Continental, another two miles southward, you might turn onto a paved side road that takes you—some 13 miles farther—into Madera Canyon, in the Santa Ritas. It's a natural recreation area, part of the Coronado National Forest, especially celebrated as a stalking ground for bird-watchers. There are public campground facilities and a small lodge and cafe. Nearby Mount Wrightson (9453 feet) has spectacular hiking trails.

Retrace your steps back to I-19, resume your journey southward, and 18 miles down the pike you reach Tubac.

This little place radiates history. It's the oldest European settlement in Arizona, tracing its beginning to 1752. In that year Spaniards established a garrison here to protect settlers and peaceful Pima and Papago Indians from raids by other Indians. Later the garrison was moved to Tucson. Tubac declined but had a brief revival when silver was discovered in the nearby mountains shortly before the Civil War. Indeed, historians count no less than eight occasions on which Tubac has withered and then revived. It is now enjoying a kind of ninth life as an art center and happy hunting ground for history buffs. With some of its original adobe walls still standing, the Tubac Presidio State Historic Park and museum tell the story in a way you can almost *feel*. There is an admission fee. Numerous shops specialize in arts and crafts.

Tubac was, incidentally, the site of the first newspaper published in Arizona. It was called *The Weekly Arizonian*.

Spanish Tradition   111

In the fertile valley between the Diablito and Santa Rita mountains the Spanish government established a presidio called Tubac in 1752. The oldest European settlement in Arizona survives today as Tubac Presidio State Historic Park. It is surrounded by a casual community of artists. (Left) Museum displays at the old Tubac Presidio. James Tallon photo

(Right) Peña Blanca Lake (White Rock) is a 52-acre aquatic jewel amidst the rugged cattle lands of southern Arizona. Anglers will enjoy fishing for bass, crappies, catfish, bluegills, and in winter the lake is stocked with rainbow trout. James Tallon photo

Equipment for the paper was laboriously hauled around Cape Horn, then transshipped by oxcart from the port of Guaymas, Mexico. Ed Cross, the editor, a bellicose type, managed to get himself embroiled in perhaps the most famous duel of territorial days. His adversary was a former Army officer named Sylvester Mowry (there's a mining ghost town named for him some miles to the east). They fought with rifles at 60 paces, and both were such sorry shots that neither got hurt. They later became fast friends, and Mowry bought the paper from Cross and moved it to Tucson.

Three miles more to the south and you're at another of the many missions established by Father Kino. Its full and proper name is Mission San José del Tumacacori. Today we call it Tumacacori National Monument.

The building you see actually was built by the Franciscan Fathers and is the successor to the original mission founded by Jesuit Father Kino. Like so many other missions of that time, it was never quite completed, and vandals and souvenir-hunters took their toll of what did survive of the handiwork of the dedicated priests. The United States government finally stepped in to care for

Tumacacori. The ruins that remain, with their graceful arches, cornices, and copings, testify to the beauty which was Tumacacori.

Ten miles south of Tumacacori State Route 289 turns off to Peña Blanca Lake, located seven miles west of the freeway in a mountain pocket of the Coronado National Forest. The lake is a mile long, and the fishing is good — bass, bluegill, crappie, catfish, and trout.

Back to I-19 and south another 8 miles, and you're at *Ambos Nogales*. They're among the larger of the several pairs of international adjoining towns lying along the United States-Mexican border. And, of these particular twins, Nogales, Mexico, is by far the larger — population 150,000 compared to 16,000 on the Arizona side.

The towns are situated in a mountain pass which, even prehistorically, was a natural pathway for commerce. And so this is a major port of entry for Mexican farm produce, livestock, and manufactured goods. (The name Nogales, by the way, comes from *nogal*, Spanish for walnut.)

What Nogales provides tourists is the chance for a quick look at Mexico without traveling to the interior. The two Nogaleses are separated only by a wire mesh

fence (without it they would be, for all practical purposes, one city). Mexicans cross the border daily to shop and work on the Arizona side, while North Americans cross to shop and dine on the Mexican side.

You can cross the border without a passport or tourist card. Some folks drive, although most park on the Arizona side and walk. Distances are short, and you spare yourself the trouble of taking out Mexican insurance at an agency on the United States side (which is always advisable when driving in Mexico). When you come back, all that's usually asked by United States immigration officials is whether you're a United States citizen. If you are going farther into Mexico you must have proof of citizenship—a voting card or birth certificate.

You can bring back $400 worth of merchandise duty-free, including one liter of spirits.

The devaluation of the peso, of course, hurt the people of Mexico and businesses on both sides of the fence. But it was a boon to the North American tourist, making Mexican pottery, silver, ceramics, and other goods more attractive values.

Let's go back to Tucson by a different route—State Route 82, northeast through Patagonia and Sonoita. The route takes you through the imposing Patagonia Mountains where, south of the little community of Patagonia, are the ghostly remnants of such old mining camps as Harshaw, Duquesne, Washington Camp, and Mowry. (Check locally for road conditions.) You look out upon a different Arizona from the one you saw driving southward from Tucson. This is grassy, cattle-grazing, rolling-hill country. (Item: The people who made the movie version of *Oklahoma!* thought this stretch of Arizona countryside looked more like Oklahoma than Oklahoma, and they shot a lot of outdoor footage here.)

Well worth a stop in Patagonia is the Museum of the Horse. It exhibits just about everything conceivable related to horses—saddles, harnesses, bridles, horseshoes, stirrups, and on and on. The items come from all over the world and date to the days of the Pony Express, the Cossacks, even to Greco-Roman times. Here, too, is the fancy velvet saddle that the Bey of Tunis gave President Franklin D. Roosevelt. There's a re-created blacksmith shop as well as a veritable fleet of old wagons—surreys, sleighs, coaches, carriages, even a hearse—and a number of Western paintings.

The moving force behind the Museum of the Horse was Anne Stradling, herself an Easterner. But she grew up loving horses, and after coming out to Arizona, did something about it. There's an admission charge.

One of the favorite spots in the state for bird-watching lies just west of Patagonia, amidst quantities of cottonwood trees that stand along Sonoita Creek. It's the Patagonia-Sonoita Creek Sanctuary, a meeting place for cold-weather birds migrating from the north and their warmer-blooded brethren flying in from the south.

Head north out of Patagonia from here. State Route 82 joins State Route 83 at Sonoita, which takes you to I-10. Twenty miles later you're in Tucson.

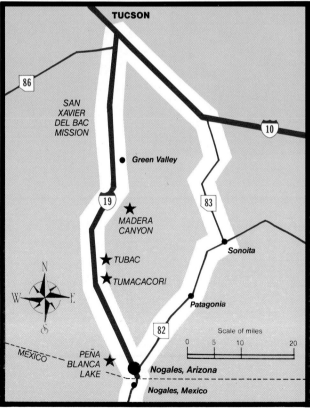

(Top) For tourists from the United States, the border crossing between the twin cities of Nogales, Arizona, and Nogales, Sonora, has long been a gateway to the charm and romance of Old Mexico.
Jeff Kida photo

(Above) The unique atmosphere of Mexico pervades many fine restaurants south of the border where mariachis serenade patrons who savor the spicy cuisine.
Jeff Kida photo

(Right) Just east of Nogales, Arizona, cottonwoods along Patagonia Creek accent the pastoral beauty of Arizona cattle country.
Gill Kenny photo

Southeastern Arizona

(Left) Untouched by progress, Ramsey Canyon in the Huachuca Mountains is a sanctuary for birds, wildlife, plants, and the people who enjoy them. Ornithologists from around the world come to the canyon to view its specialty — hummingbirds.
Willis Peterson photo

(Above) Fort Huachuca, at the mouth of Huachuca Canyon, has spanned the years from horse-mounted troopers communicating with bugle and signal flags to the most current electronic advances of the space age. Established in the turbulent days of the Indian Wars of the 1870s, Fort Huachuca today is a major Army installation dealing in communications. Alan Benoit photo

The southeastern corner of our state is, historically, Arizona at its rip-roaringest! It's where the Earps and Clantons took a quick bead on each other at the OK Corral...where Cochise and Geronimo, those doughty warriors of the Chiricahua Apaches, stood stubbornly against the implacable might of the United States Cavalry...and where the town of Douglas was pelted with stray bullets from a Mexican revolutionary battle fought in neighboring Agua Prieta.

Southeastern Arizona has all this shoot-'em-up history—and, to boot, some spectacular high-desert valleys that seem to have no horizon...and quiet, verdant canyons offering sanctuary to the migrant bird and camera-hunting bird-watcher.

This is all one county—Cochise County—and it's well worth two or three days of your traveling time, although you can touch down at major way stations in one.

Start from Tucson, head east on Interstate 10, and 42 miles farther near Benson turn south on State Route 90 to Sierra Vista. It's a vibrant and vital community, made so by the presence of Fort Huachuca, home of the Army Strategic Communications Command and electronics proving ground. There's a museum, this being the nation's only active surviving cavalry post (it was established in 1877 to fight the Apaches and shield the region from possible Mexican incursions), and admission is free.

Another attraction is the Ramsey Canyon bird sanctuary, famous for its hummingbirds. It's six miles south of town and four miles into the Huachuca Mountains. It is owned by The Nature Conservancy, a national organization dedicated to preserving natural habitats. The preserve is small. Parking is extremely limited. And too many visitors at one time scare the hummers away. So the caretakers suggest you telephone first to schedule a visit, and avoid weekends. Admission is free, but no picnicking, please. (You can do that in numerous other canyons of the Huachuca Mountains.)

A third attraction is the Coronado National Memorial (south on State Route 92 for a distance of 17 miles to Montezuma Canyon Road, then six miles to the Memorial). It's near the point where Francisco Vásquez de Coronado

entered what is now the United States in 1540 and thus commemorates the first major expedition of Europeans into the present-day Southwest.

The Memorial offers a natural cul-de-sac for hiking and birding. A stirring overlook into Mexico rewards more adventuresome visitors. Friendly rangers staff an interpretive center and rest station. Seldom is the Memorial crowded, even on weekends — a perfect sanctuary of peace and quiet.

Back to Sierra Vista and east on State Route 90 some 20 miles to U.S. Route 80. Head north 15 miles to Tombstone, surely the most famous of all Western towns.

What strikes some first-time visitors to Tombstone is the fact that it doesn't have the varnished and restored look of so many historic places. Remarkably, it appears pretty much as it must have a hundred years ago…but with paved streets and power poles, of course. It's not a fancy town: simple wooden buildings and the like, but isn't that the way frontier towns looked?

The famous places are all still there, waiting to be seen — the OK Corral, Boothill Cemetery, Bird Cage Theater, the *Tombstone Epitaph*, the courthouse (now a state historic park), and the Crystal Palace Saloon, watering place of such distinguished local gentry as Wyatt Earp, Bat Masterson, Johnny Ringo, and Doc Holiday. The best way to see all this is to pick up a brochure and map at the Tombstone Chamber of Commerce and take a self-guided walking tour. The historic section of town comprises a compact 10 blocks or so. A good place to start the tour is Schieffelin Hall, where you can watch a 45-minute film.

Ed Schieffelin was the prospector who made the big silver find that brought 10,000 people—including the celebrated roughnecks—to Tombstone. "All you'll find in those hills is your tombstone," Schieffelin was warned. And Tombstone it became.

If you time your Tombstone visit right, you can catch its big annual celebration, Helldorado Days, along about mid-October. It's full of Tombstone-style bang-bang—a reenactment of the Earp-Clanton gun battle at the OK Corral, a fast draw contest (Tombstone says it's the oldest annual competition of its kind in the country), and a replay of the shooting of Marshal White. Much of the fun takes place in a roped-off section of historic Allen Street.

Some of the sight-seeing spots in Tombstone charge admission.

Backtrack down U.S. Route 80 some 24 miles to Bisbee. You'll enter it through Mule Pass Tunnel, the state's longest (one-third mile), and find that Bisbee is a larger and newer version of Jerome (see Tour 6)—a sort of ghost town-that-won't-give-in-to-the-ghosts. Phelps Dodge Corporation copper operations closed down in the mid-1970s. Bisbee, instead of drying up and blowing away, launched a new career as a tourist attraction and a mile-high refuge for retirees and other folks hankering after its just-about-perfect climate and late 19th century atmosphere.

Spread out willy-nilly along the gullies and ravines of Mule Mountain, Bisbee still bears an extraordinary resemblance to its historical self. In the heart of the old downtown is the rococo anachronism known as the Copper Queen Hotel, once one of the swankiest hostelries to be found between Los Angeles and El Paso. It is restored and fully

(Far left) On May 1, 1880, the Tombstone Epitaph put out its first edition. Depending on what you want to believe, the newspaper gained its unusual name either because "newspapers, like epitaphs, usually don't tell the truth," or merely because the title seemed appropriate to a journal chronicling the events happening in a town called Tombstone.
Suzanne Clemenz photo

(Left) Details surrounding the showdown at the OK Corral are legend, and have become part of Tombstone's claim to fame as "the town too tough to die."
Ed Cooper photo

(Right) Brewery Gulch looks much as it did in the days when the town was a rugged mining camp. In the distance is the colorful Lavender Pit that helped make Bisbee a great copper center.
Josef Muench photo

(Following panel) Stone columns of the Chiricahua National Monument in southeastern Arizona.
Jeff Gnass photo

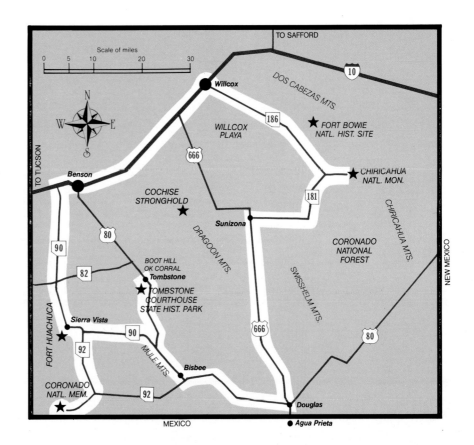

operative, complete with sidewalk cafe. (Theodore Roosevelt once stayed here, and so did General John J. Pershing, when he invaded Mexico in pursuit of Pancho Villa.) Nearby is the Mining and Historical Museum, once the general offices of Phelps Dodge, with all kinds of equipment, a mine diorama, and the like. (Free admission.) Next door is the classically handsome Covenant Presbyterian Church, built in 1903, and copied after an ancient European church. And then there's Brewery Gulch, which, when Bisbee was in its prime, around 1900, and had a population of 25,000, helped local miners dispose of their earnings in its 40 saloons, brothels, and gambling houses. Today's Brewery Gulch is noted for its potpourri of shops and art galleries.

And, finally, up in the canyons are Bisbee's turn-of-the-century houses, squeezed into odd lots, some on streets so steep that the postmen won't deliver mail to them.

The really big attractions, though, are the mines—the great Lavender Pit (named not for its color but for a mine manager named Harry Lavender) and the underground Copper Queen. You can tour the pit by bus and take a trip into the Queen on a narrow-gauge train (after being properly outfitted with hard hat, slicker, and lamp). Also available is a minibus tour into the historical section of Bisbee. There are charges for the tours.

Leaving Bisbee, return to U.S. Route 80 and head east to Douglas (24 miles) and its across-the-fence Mexican neighbor, Agua Prieta. Not large as border towns go, Agua Prieta offers a slower pace, authentic Mexican food, and bargains in leather goods, spirits, and fabrics.

Douglas, like Bisbee, can also boast of some spirited history: the time Pancho Villa tried to take Agua Prieta, for example, and bullets flew into Douglas. Or the time when Aimee Semple McPherson, famous Los Angeles evangelist in the 1920s, vanished into the ocean off California and walked into Douglas from the desert, saying she'd been kidnaped and held near Agua Prieta. And then there was the presence, in the 1960s, of the well-known author, Thornton Wilder. Wilder spent 18 months in Douglas, writing his novel *The Eighth Day*. He lived at the Gadsden Hotel (which has some anachronistic elegance in its own ornate lobby dominated by four rose-colored marble columns), and was often seen tooling around town in his black Thunderbird.

Pick up U.S. Route 666 from Douglas, and some 30 miles to the north it connects with State Route 181 which leads you into a unique Western landscape known as the Chiricahua National Monument.

It comprises 17 square miles on the west side of the Chiricahua Mountains and is widely known as the Wonderland of Rocks. Volcanic eruptions, followed by milleniums of erosion, created a maze of rock formations, many of them strange and dramatic. They've acquired names like China Boy, Punch and Judy, the Sea Captain, and Organ Pipe Formation.

Pay an admission fee at the visitors center and then you can drive through the monument on a six-and-a-half-mile road to a place called Massai Point. It gives you a view of the rocks and a long look at two lovely valleys—Sulphur Springs, on the west, and San Simon, on the east. On your way back, turnouts along the road have signs identi-

fying some of the rock formations. Excellent hiking trails provide access to more. There's a campground in Bonita Canyon, a half-mile or so from the visitors center.

As you tour the monument, you might bear in mind that you're trodding on historic soil. This was the mountain home of the famous Apaches Cochise and Geronimo. Cochise, in fact, is memorialized in stone—a rock formation just north of the monument called Cochise Head.

Cochise's great fortress in those years of the Indian wars, however, was the east face of the Dragoon Mountains, just to the west of the Chiricahaus. It's known as Cochise Stronghold, reachable via a dirt road that takes off from U.S. Route 666 about 10 miles northwest of its intersection with the highway to the national monument. What you see today is almost precisely what Cochise saw a century ago: a natural rocky fortress with countless points of vantage atop rock pinnacles. But where Apache wickiups once stood, there is now a campground and picnic area. Cochise, incidentally, is buried somewhere in that impregnable fortress...but nobody knows where.

Go westward out of the Chiricahua monument and then northwestward via State Route 186 toward Willcox. En route, if you feel hardy enough, take the road to Fort Bowie National Historic Site. In its day, Bowie was the major military post protecting settlers and travelers from marauding Apaches. The Butterfield Stage Line ran between Tucson and the fort. What a precarious route that was! A stage line that traveled the road after the Butterfield Stage was discontinued had 22 of its drivers killed by Cochise and his men over a 16-month period. The adobe ruins of Fort Bowie can still be seen. A dirt road runs about 10 miles east of State Route 186. Then you have to walk about a mile and a half. A National Park Service ranger is on duty from 8 a.m. to 5 p.m.

On to Willcox and then back to Tucson via I-10 (distance from Willcox: 80 miles).

Hiking Arizona

These hikes cover a variety of beautiful areas and will appeal to anyone interested in the out-of-doors. There are mountain hikes and desert ones; wilderness experiences and adventures in metropolitan areas. Some are easy, others modestly difficult, and a few will challenge even the toughest backpacker.

WHITE HOUSE RUIN IN CANYON DE CHELLY

Location: Two miles east of Chinle to the Park Service Visitors Center. Take the South Rim Drive 6.8 miles to White House Ruin Overlook. (In tour 2 area.)

Description: Sandstone cliffs hundreds of feet high, erosion-sculptured rocks, and magnificent ruins of a prehistoric culture. This one-and-one-quarter-mile trail is the only canyon trail you may hike without a guide.

Degree of difficulty and time required: Modest; one-and-one-half to two hours.

Best time of year: June through October.

BRIGHT ANGEL TRAIL IN GRAND CANYON

Location: Seventy-eight miles northwest of Flagstaff on U. S. Route 180 at Grand Canyon Village. (In tour 3 area.)

Description: Bright Angel must be considered among America's best and most popular trails. It is nine-and-one-half spectacular miles from the trail head to Bright Angel campground at the bottom of the Canyon. Reservations are required for camping below the rim. Write to Back Country Reservations Office (address on page 126).

Degree of difficulty and time required: Difficult; two days.

Alternate day hikes: Bright Angel Trail to Indian Gardens is nine miles round trip, and takes all day. The South Kaibab Trail to Cedar Ridge is three miles round trip and takes one-half day. The South Kaibab hike provides a very dramatic view of the Canyon, but there is no water along the trail. Both hikes are difficult.

Best time of year: May through October.

ISLAND TRAIL IN WALNUT CANYON

Location: Five miles east of Flagstaff on Interstate 40, then three miles south to Walnut Canyon National Monument. (In tour 3 area.)

Description: Two-hundred-forty stairs and a paved trail three-fourths of a mile long lead to 25-30 individual prehistoric Indian ruins. The beautiful canyon has a mixture of vegetation from prickly pear cactus to ponderosa pine. Note: the elevation is 6800 feet.

Degree of difficulty and time required: Easy; one hour.

Best time of year: May through October

LAVA FLOW TRAIL AT SUNSET CRATER

Location: Thirteen miles northeast of Flagstaff on U. S. Route 89 in Sunset Crater National Monument. (In tour 3 area.) **Description:** A different experience, on and under the earth. This half-mile trail through a vast cinder area includes some novel volcanic features, such as squeeze-ups and a lava tube (sometimes called an ice cave) which those with flashlights can explore.

Degree of difficulty and time required: Easy; one and one-half hours.

Best time of year: April through October.

PALM CANYON

Location: Sixty-three miles north of Yuma on U. S. Route 95, then east on seven miles of dirt road to the trail head. (In tour 4 area.)

Description: A delightful half-mile hike on the Sonoran Desert, with interesting flora and fauna, into the rugged canyons of the Kofa Mountains, with clusters of Arizona's only native palm trees.

Degree of difficulty and time required: Modest; two hours.

Best time of year: November through April.

HAVASUPAI CANYON

Location: Fifty-five miles northeast of Kingman on old U. S. Route 66, then north 60 miles on Indian Route 18 to Hualapai Hilltop parking area. (Near tour 5 area.)

Description: Located in a remote area of the Grand Canyon, Havasupai Canyon has often been called Shangri-la because of its high waterfalls, turquoise-colored pools, and beautiful scenery. Ten-mile trail from parking area to campground.

Notice: This is the home of the Havasupai Indians. Because space in the canyon is limited, permits *must* be acquired in advance! Contact Supai Enterprises (602) 448-2121.

Degree of difficulty and time required: Difficult; two days.

Added option: Nine beautiful, but difficult, miles beyond the campground is the Colorado River. Allow another day or two.

Best time of year: May through October.

THREE IN ONE—PETRIFIED FOREST

Location: Twenty-five miles east of Holbrook on Interstate 40. (In tour 7 area.)

Description: Blue Mesa—a photographer's delight in a lunar-like landscape. A colorfully eroded cross section of the Painted Desert. Crystal Forest—perhaps the most picturesque collection of petrified wood in the world. Long Logs—looks like a 200-million-year-old log jam. Some petrified trees over 170-feet long. Each hike is approximately three-fourths of a mile long on a paved loop trail.

Degree of difficulty and time required: Easy; one hour each.

Best time of year: April through October, but park is open all year.

TONTO NATURAL BRIDGE

Location: Ten miles north of Payson on State Route 87. (In tour 7 area.)

Description: Located on private land. The three-fourths of a mile trail from the small 1920s lodge, along the creek to the world's largest travertine natural bridge, is like fantasyland — an ivy-draped ravine with travertine-formed caves, and cool shaded pools. Bring a picnic lunch.

Degree of difficulty and time required: Modest; two hours.

Best time of year: May through October.

WEAVERS NEEDLE, SUPERSTITION MOUNTAINS

Location: Approximately seven miles south of Apache Junction on U.S. Route 60, then east on Peralta Road (gravel) three miles to the Dons Club base camp and trail head. (In tour 8 area.)

Description: Rugged desert mountain terrain. This is the area of the Superstition Mountains most prominently mentioned in stories of the fabled Lost Dutchman gold mine.

Degree of difficulty and time required: Difficult; one day.

Alternate: Another excellent hike is to Miners Needle. Trailhead is in the same area as Weavers Needle. Hike does not include as much climbing.

Degree of difficulty and time required: Modest; one day.

Best time of year: November through April.

SQUAW PEAK AND SOUTH MOUNTAIN PARKS

Location: Squaw Peak Park — Located in the Phoenix Mountain Preserve north of Lincoln Drive between 16th and 24th streets, on Squaw Peak Drive. South Mountain Park — South on Central Avenue to its end at South Mountain Park. (In tour 9 area.)

Descriptions: Squaw Peak Park — a good range of hikes available, from leisurely to difficult. Summit Trail is difficult, but very popular with joggers. The view of the city is exceptional. South Mountain — the largest municipal park in the world, over 16,000 acres. Pick up an illustrated brochure with trail maps at the park entrance. Also, there are stables in the area should you prefer riding the trails.

Degree of difficulty and time required: Both variable.

Best time of year: October through May.

SHEEP CROSSING AND MOUNT BALDY

Location: Between McNary and Springerville, on State Route 260, then south on State Route 273 approximately seven miles (dirt road beyond Sunrise Lake), then turn west one mile to parking area at Sheep Crossing. (In tour 10 area.)

Description: Excellent alpine hiking, 8000 feet throughout the Sheep Crossing area along the West Fork of the Little Colorado. Sheep Crossing is also the trailhead for the hike to the top of Mount Baldy. It is seven miles one way; elevation is 11,590 feet. Frequent afternoon thunderstorms occur all summer.

Notice: The very top of the mountain is on the Fort Apache Indian Reservation, and considered sacred. No trespassing!

Degree of difficulty and time required: Mount Baldy, difficult; two days.

Best time of year: Sheep Crossing area, June through September. Mount Baldy hike, July through August.

PICACHO PEAK

Location: Approximately 40 miles northwest of downtown Tucson on Interstate 10 to Picacho Peak State Park. (Near tour 13 area.)

Description: There are several interesting trails meandering through the desert vegetation and boulders of this volcanic remnant. In spring, following rainy winters, the desert slopes are covered with a carpet of golden poppies. The trail to the top is steep, but quite hikeable.

Degree of difficulty and time required: Climb to top difficult; one-half day. Other trails in the area are variable, set your own pace.

Best time of year: October through May. Poppies are generally best from the last week of March through the first week of April.

SABINO CANYON

Location: Northeast of Tucson in Santa Catalina Mountains. (In tour 14 area.)

Description: A desert refuge of streams and waterfalls in the mountain foothills. Drive to visitors center, take a tram into the canyon, and hike out. Also, there are many good hiking and biking trails in the area.

Degree of difficulty and time required: Easy; two hours.

Best time of year: October through May.

ECHO CANYON IN THE CHIRICAHUAS

Location: Approximately 33 miles southeast of Willcox on State Route 186 to Chiricahua National Monument. (In tour 16 area.)

Description: A "wonderland of rocks," the name for another area of the Chiricahua National Monument, could actually apply to the entire mountain chain. Extraordinary weathered rock sculptures make the Echo Canyon Trail a photographic delight. Numerous other exceptional hikes in the area. Elevation is 4500 feet.

Degree of difficulty and time required: Modest; three hours.

Best time of year: May through October.

For More Information

APACHE/SITGREAVES NATIONAL FOREST
P. O. Box 640
Springerville, AZ 85938
(602) 333-4301

ARIZONA GAME & FISH DEPARTMENT
2222 West Greenway Road
Phoenix, AZ 85023
(602) 942-3000

ARIZONA OFFICE OF TOURISM
1480 East Bethany Home Road
Phoenix, AZ 85014
(602) 255-3618

ARIZONA DEPARTMENT OF PUBLIC SAFETY
Road Conditions — State & Federal
(602) 262-8261
Highway Patrol
(602) 262-8011

ARIZONA STATE PARKS
1688 West Adams
Phoenix, AZ 85007
(602) 255-4174

BUREAU OF LAND MANAGEMENT
3707 North Seventh Street
Phoenix, AZ 85014
(602) 241-5504

CANYON DE CHELLY TOUR CONCESSIONAIRE
Thunderbird Tours
P. O. Box 548
Chinle, AZ 86503
(602) 674-5443

COCONINO NATIONAL FOREST
2323 East Greenlaw Lane
Flagstaff, AZ 86001
(602) 527-7400

CORONADO NATIONAL FOREST
Federal Building
301 West Congress
Tucson, AZ 85701
(602) 629-6483

GRAND CANYON BELOW THE RIM CAMPING
Back Country Reservations
Grand Canyon National Park
P. O. Box 129
Grand Canyon, AZ 86023

GRAND CANYON NORTH RIM CONCESSIONAIRE
TW Services, Inc.
P.O. Box 400
Cedar City, UT 84720
(602) 638-2611 — Arizona
(801) 586-7686 — Utah

GRAND CANYON SOUTH RIM CONCESSIONAIRE
Grand Canyon Lodges
P.O. Box 699
Grand Canyon, AZ 86023
(602) 638-2401 — Arizona
(602) 952-1212 — Phoenix only
(800) 528-0483 — Outside Arizona
(800) 221-5599 — Arizona Toll Free

KAIBAB NATIONAL FOREST
800 South Sixth Street
Williams, AZ 86046
(602) 635-2681

LAKE POWELL CONCESSIONAIRE
Del Webb Recreational Properties
P.O. Box 29040
Phoenix, AZ 85038
(602) 278-8888 — Arizona
(800) 258-6154 — Outside Arizona

METROPOLITAN TUCSON CONVENTION & VISITORS BUREAU
450 West Paseo Redondo
Suite 110
Tucson, AZ 85705
(602) 624-1817

NATIONAL PARKS & MONUMENTS
1115 North First Street
Phoenix, AZ 85004
(602) 261-4956

PHOENIX & VALLEY OF THE SUN CONVENTION & VISITORS BUREAU
505 North Second Street
Suite 300
Phoenix, AZ 85004
(602) 254-6500

PRESCOTT NATIONAL FOREST
344 South Cortez
Prescott, AZ 86301
(602) 445-1762

TONTO NATIONAL FOREST
P. O. Box 29070
2324 East McDowell Road
Phoenix, AZ 85038
(602) 225-5200

HIGHWAY SAFETY TIPS

Sudden desert dust storms occur often in Arizona during spring and summer months, reducing visibility and frequently bringing heavy rain. During storms drivers should proceed cautiously with lights on. If visibility worsens, it's advisable to drive well off the highway and *turn off* the car lights. Normally dry washes can become hazardous from a storm miles away as rain causes flash floods downstream. The Arizona Highway Patrol is available for urgent medical care, mechanical assistance, or simply directions. An officer can be summoned by telephoning one of three numbers: Phoenix — 262-8011; Tucson — 746-1421; Flagstaff — 774-4561.

Index

(Pages with pictures set in **bold** type.)

128 Index

(Back cover) Late summer thunderstorms often provide dazzling electrical displays in Saguaro National Monument near Tucson. Willard Clay photo

Share the <u>Arizona Highways</u> adventures...

with a special gift subscription offer.

Share the adventures captured every month in *Arizona Highways Magazine*, the nation's premier state publication. Send an *Arizona Highways* gift subscription.

Order a one-year subscription at the regular $15 rate, and each additional one-year gift is only $13. If not already a subscriber, become one for a year ($15), two years ($25), or three years ($35). Each one-year gift: $13. You can even extend your own subscription and order gifts for only $13.

Arizona Highways Magazine — a gift sure to be appreciated all through the year for its beauty and for your thoughtfulness in giving it!

Arizona Landmarks

Arizona is a land of landmarks. And this magnificent book takes you there in pictures and an easy-reading text seasoned with anecdotes, tall tales, frontier humor, and fascinating history. You'll travel the deserts, mountains, canyons, and plateaus — across lakes, down rivers, through Indian ruins, and modern cities. We've covered them all in 160 pages and over 180 full-color photographs in a book 10 by 13 inches in size. It's a remarkable journey through space and time!

$35 — Hardcover

Outdoors In Arizona
A Guide to Fishing and Hunting

No more guessing where to find Arizona's best fishing and hunting spots. In this new 192-page guidebook, Arizona fishing and hunting authority Bob Hirsch reveals secrets he's learned during a lifetime in the Arizona outdoors. To help plan your trips, the guidebook divides Arizona into ten regions — then covers each region in detail with a full-color map, tips on best fishing spots, and where game is most likely to be found. Illustrated with more than 150 photographs and reproduced in magnificent *Arizona Highways* color — plus sketches and paintings by famed wildlife artist Larry Toschik.

$12.95 — Softcover

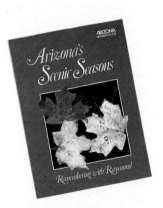

Arizona's Scenic Seasons
Remembering with Raymond

You'll be spellbound by the words of *Arizona Highways'* famed editor Raymond Carlson and captivated by more than 100 spectacular full-color photographs in this unique chronicle of Arizona's changing seasons. For Carlson, recording Arizona's seasons was "more than a job — it is a crusade." 128 pages. 100 photographs.

$11.50 — Softcover

Travel Arizona

Now you know why *Travel Arizona* has become the state's most popular travel guide. This is a good time to share your enjoyment with friends and relatives. Packed with full-color photography and maps, the 128-page book makes an ideal gift.

$8.95 — Softcover

Laminated map

We've taken our popular Arizona road map, printed it flat — then laminated it front and back in clear plastic for durability and wipe-clean convenience. Now it's ready to hang, framed or unframed, on your home or office wall as a handsome reference and trip-planning aid. 24 by 36 inches in size.

$5.75

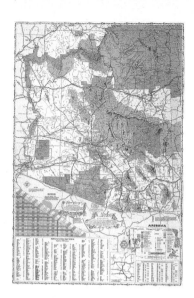

Note cards

Now your personal correspondence can carry two messages — your own and Arizona's. Each *Arizona Highways* note card features a stunning Arizona scene on the front reproduced in full color. Inside pages are blank for your personal note writing. Cards measure 5½ by 4½ inches (folded) and come with matching envelopes. Each box contains ten cards with two different photographs, plus ten envelopes.

$4.75 — per box

Box A
Hedgehog Cactus on the Sonora Desert
Larry Ulrich

Saguaros at Sunset on the Desert West of Tucson
Peter Kresan

Box B
Rainbow over Red Rock Country Oak Creek Canyon
Dick Canby

Poppy Spread — Ajo Mountains Organ Pipe Cactus National Monument
David Muench

 **Order Form** — Prices subject to change

Mail order form to: Arizona Highways
2039 West Lewis Avenue
Phoenix, Arizona 85009

Orders also can be placed by calling (602) 258-1000 or toll-free within Arizona: 1-800-543-5432

All prices include postage and handling.

QTY	ITEM	ITEM #	PRICE EA.	TOTAL
	Outdoors in Arizona: A Guide to Fishing and Hunting Available after 1/15/86 — Softcover	OFHS5	$12.95	
	Note cards — Box A	NOTS4	4.75	
	Note cards — Box B	NOTS5	4.75	
	Laminated map	LAMAP	5.75	
	Arizona Landmarks — Hardcover	ARLH5	35.00	
	Arizona's Scenic Seasons — Softcover	SEBS4	11.50	
	Travel Arizona — Softcover	TABS5	8.95	
	1-Year Subscription	SUB01	15.00	
	2-Year Subscription	SUB02	25.00	
	3-Year Subscription	SUB03	35.00	
	Additional 1-Year Gifts	SUB15	13.00	
	Foreign Subscriptions (per year)	SUBF1	18.00	
			TOTAL	

Complete this box for all orders:

My Name _____

Address _____

City _____ State _____ Zip _____

If your order includes a subscription for yourself, is it ☐ New ☐ Extension

☐ Payment enclosed   Charge my ☐ MasterCard   ☐ VISA

Credit card number _____   Expiration date _____

Gift recipient:

SEND ITEM(S) # _____

To: _____

Address _____

City _____ State _____ Zip _____

The first issue of new subscriptions will be mailed within six weeks of order receipt. Allow six weeks for delivery of other items.

TAZ105

Detach Here